Ministerial Priesthood
in the Third Millennium

Ministerial Priesthood in the Third Millennium

Faithfulness of Christ, Faithfulness of Priests

LITURGICAL PRESS
Collegeville, Minnesota

www.litpress.org

Cover design by Ann Blattner.

5   6   7   8   9

Library of Congress Cataloging-in-Publication Data

Ministerial priesthood in the third millennium : faithfulness of Christ, faithfulness of priests / Ronald D. Witherup . . . [et al.].
    p.   cm.
    Includes bibliographical references.
    ISBN 978-0-8146-3326-7 — ISBN 978-0-8146-3901-6 (e-book)
    1. Pastoral theology—Catholic Church—Congresses.   2. Catholic Church—Clergy—Congresses.   3. Priesthood—Catholic Church—Congresses.   4. Priests—Congresses.   I. Witherup, Ronald D., 1950–

BX1913.M553 2009
253.088'282—dc22   2009042370

Contents

v

vi   *Ministerial Priesthood in the Third Millennium*

Contributors

Monsignor Kevin Irwin is a priest of the Archdiocese of New York who is dean of the School of Theology and Religious Studies at The Catholic University of America. He received his master's degree from the University of Notre Dame and his doctorate of theology from Pontificio Istituto Liturgico, Collegio Sant' Anselmo, Rome. He holds the Walter J. Schmitz Chair of Liturgical Studies and has authored fourteen books on liturgy and sacraments. In addition to his academic work Monsignor Irwin regularly celebrates Mass and preaches at the Basilica of the National Shrine of the Immaculate Conception in Washington DC during the week.

Monsignor Paul G. McPartlan is a priest of the Archdiocese of Westminster (UK) and Carl J. Peter Professor of Systematic Theology and Ecumenism at The Catholic University of America. He was born in Newcastle upon Tyne and graduated from Cambridge in mathematics in 1978. Having studied philosophy and theology at the Pontifical Gregorian University in Rome, he was ordained a priest by Cardinal Basil Hume in 1984. He gained his doctorate from Oxford and then served for four years in a London parish. After holding a postdoctoral research fellowship at St. Edmund's College, Cambridge, from 1993–1995, he was appointed to the faculty of Heythrop College in the University of London where he taught systematic theology for ten years before coming to CUA in 2005. He is a member of the International Theological Commission and a member also of the international commissions for theological dialogue between the Roman Catholic Church and the Orthodox Church, and the Roman Catholic Church and the World Methodist Council, respectively.

Very Rev. Lawrence B. Terrien, SS, is a former superior general of the Society of St. Sulpice and the first American to be elected to that position. He is an alumnus of Theological College and served as rector of the seminary from 1986 to 1992. He has a doctorate of sacred theology from the Catholic University of Leuven. Father Terrien has served as associate professor of systematic theology, academic dean, and vice-rector at St. Patrick's Seminary in Menlo Park, CA. He has also been dean of the ecclesiastical faculty of theology at Saint Mary's Seminary & University in Baltimore. He is presently professor of systematic theology at Saint Mary's Seminary & University.

Rev. Michael Witczak is an assistant professor of liturgical studies at The Catholic University of America and specializes in the history and theology of eucharistic celebration, sacramental liturgy, history of liturgy, and liturgical celebration of the saints. He previously served as a professor of liturgical studies, vice-rector, and then rector of Saint Francis Seminary in Saint Francis, WI. He is a priest of the Archdiocese of Milwaukee and for many years wrote a column for priests in the archdiocesan quarterly liturgy newsletter. He holds a doctorate in sacred liturgy from the Pontifical Liturgical Institute in Rome. Father Witczak is a member of the North American Academy of Liturgy, Societas Liturgica, the Catholic Theological Society of America, the Society for Catholic Liturgy, the Henry Bradshaw Society for the editing of rare liturgical texts, and the Alcuin Club. He was awarded the Archbishop's Vatican II Award for Service in Liturgy in 2001 and the Salesianum Alumni Association Sal Terrae Award for Service to the Church in 2007.

Very Rev. Ronald D. Witherup, SS, is superior general of the Society of St. Sulpice, known as the Sulpicians, an order of diocesan priests dedicated to initial and ongoing formation of priests. Father Witherup previously served eleven years as provincial of the Sulpicians' U.S. Province. A former academic dean and professor of Sacred Scripture at St. Patrick Seminary in Menlo Park, CA, he holds a doctorate in biblical studies from Union Theological Seminary in Richmond, VA. He is a frequent retreat master for priests and deacons, and he often lectures on biblical and theological topics. Among his many publications are: *101 Questions & Answers on Paul* (Paulist, 2003), *Scripture: Dei Verbum* (Paulist, 2006), *St. Paul: Called to Conversion* (St. Anthony Messenger, 2007), and *Stations of the Cross According to Saint Paul* (Paulist, 2008). He produced a set of CDs for the Year of Paul, titled *Saint Paul: His Life, Faith and Writings* (NowYouKnowMedia, 2008), and he coedited the recent book, *The Four Gospels: Catholic Personal Study Edition* (Liturgical Press, 2009).

Introduction

Monsignor Kevin W. Irwin

If you Google the word "symposium," in .07 seconds you receive 56,700,000 possible hits, the first one being (of course!) a Wikipedia article. That article indicates that the word "symposium" means to come together for a discussion, or an academic conference. Later on the article indicates that another meaning of "symposium" is "to drink together"!—meaning that the kind of conversation at a symposium is meant to be relaxed and convivial.

When we at The Catholic University of America first learned of Pope Benedict XVI's intention to proclaim a "Year for Priests" we decided that we should do what a Catholic university does best—host a symposium to engage participants in discussion and dialogue with presenters and with each other. The aim is to offer an academic symposium that has pastoral implications for the ordained, for seminarians, and the baptized faithful with whom we work and minister in our various apostolates and parishes. In effect the symposium mirrors what we have always done at CUA in cooperation with Theological College and the eight other houses of formation with whom we collaborate in DC. We at the university provide the academic courses in theology, philosophy, and canon law for our students (including courses in supervising ministry, pastoral theology, preaching, presiding at sacraments, etc.) and cooperate with the formators at the formation houses where the students "unpack" what they have learned and apply their learning to pastoral placements and eventually to their (largely parish) assignments.

This book collects the backbone of the symposium—the academic papers presented. Unfortunately it does not (and cannot!) contain the discussions both at the symposium itself or the informal conversations had over coffee or lunch or at the events surrounding Theological College's alumni days. But we judged early on that if we could publish these papers we would make a particular, university-based contribution to the Year for Priests. We cannot thank the staff of Liturgical Press enough for working with us so closely in such a short time to produce this volume.

The range of issues about the priesthood presented here reflect the range of issues faced by the (American) priest today. The presenters are all acknowledged scholars and professors. They are also ordained and ministering priests. They bring to their craft of doing academic theology the lens offered by pastoral ministry. Hence they are particularly qualified to speak to the topics at hand.

The Sulpician Superior General Rev. Ron Witherup, SS, sets the tone by reminding us all—lay and ordained—that Christ is our one high priest and that through baptism and ordination we all participate in that unique and eternal priesthood. Msgr. Paul McPartlan offers rich insight about the terminology we use to describe "the priest" and nuances our understandings of them and of the ministry of the priest through them. The former Sulpician Superior General Rev. Lawrence Terrien, SS, reflects briefly on the particular contribution of the French school of priestly spirituality as he proceeds to digest and comment on contemporary magisterial documents on the priesthood and their immediate implications for priests today. Rev. Michael Witczak follows in a long tradition of liturgical scholars at CUA by emphasizing the theological meaning of the liturgy we celebrate—*lex orandi, lex credendi*—with specific reference to the present rites of ordination. My own contribution follows something of a trajectory in my own research and writing in raising the perennial question about what are the spiritual and daily life implications of celebrating the liturgy for and with the people of Christ?

Allow me to conclude by inviting you, the reader of these papers, to engage afresh the ideas offered here and reflect on them for your own priesthood—baptized and ordained—for your sake, for all our sakes, for the sake of the church, and in particular for those who are ordained priests and serve the church in this third millennium.

Chapter 1

The Biblical Foundations of the Priesthood: The Contribution of Hebrews[1]

Very Rev. Ronald D. Witherup, SS

The word that one most often encounters when reading about the Letter to the Hebrews is "mysterious."[2] It is an apt description for this neglected letter of the New Testament, which is at once both intriguing and difficult to understand. To read Hebrews is to enter into an astonishing world of divine beings and hyperbole.

---

1. The following abbreviations are used in this essay: AB (Anchor Bible); *ABD* [*The Anchor Bible Dictionary*, 6 vols. (New York: Doubleday, 1992)]; *Bib* (*Biblica*); CCC (*Catechism of the Catholic Church*, 2nd ed. [Libreria Editrice Vaticana, 1997]); *EDNT* (*Exegetical Dictionary of the New Testament* [Grand Rapids: Eerdmans, 1991]); JSNTSS (Journal for the Study of the New Testament Supplement Series); *LG* (*Lumen Gentium*, Vatican II's Dogmatic Constitution on the Church [1964]); NAB (New American Bible with Revised New Testament [1989]); NRSV (New Revised Standard Version: Catholic Edition [1991]); *PDV* (*Pastores Dabo Vobis*, John Paul II's Apostolic Exhortation on Priestly Formation [1992]); *PO* (*Presbyterorum Ordinis*, Vatican Council II's Decree on the Ministry and Life of Priests [1965]); SBL (Studies in Biblical Literature); *ScriptBull* (*Scripture Bulletin*); SubBi (Subsidia Biblica); *TDNT* (*Theological Dictionary of the New Testament* [Grand Rapids: Eerdmans, 1995]); *TDOT* (*Theological Dictionary of the Old Testament* [Grand Rapids: Eerdmans, 1991]).

2. I extend sincere gratitude to Very Rev. David M. O'Connell, CM, president of The Catholic University of America, and to Rev. Melvin C. Blanchette, SS, rector of Theological College, for their gracious invitation to participate in this symposium. I also thank Rev. Msgr. Paul J. Langsfeld for several helpful comments in the preparation of this paper.

One gets the sense of standing on the threshold of the cosmos. The very first words of the letter set this cosmic tone: "In times past, God spoke in partial and various ways to our ancestors through the prophets; in these last days, he spoke to us through a son, whom he made heir of all things and through whom he created the universe" (Heb 1:1-2, NAB).[3]

Yet there can be no doubt that this letter, more than any other writing of the New Testament, has contributed to the Catholic Church's understanding of the priesthood. Its unique presentation of Jesus Christ as the great High Priest has inspired Christians through the ages to reflect upon what God has given the world in the gift of his own Son. In keeping with the theme of this symposium during this unprecedented year for priests proclaimed by Pope Benedict XVI, I propose to explore the fundamental contribution of Hebrews and how it might apply pastorally to the priesthood in the third millennium.

My lecture comprises four parts: the context of Hebrews and why it matters; the principal message of the letter regarding Jesus Christ, the High Priest; the influence of Hebrews on the church's theology of the priesthood; and proposed reflections on the pastoral application of this letter today.

The Context of Hebrews and Why It Matters

If Hebrews has generally been a neglected book of the New Testament, recent publications in English have begun to remedy this situation. There are now several outstanding English commentaries and monographs on the letter that provide a rich collection of resources from which to seek guidance as one enters the world of Hebrews.[4] At the outset, I should state clearly some

---

3. Except where indicated otherwise, the biblical quotations are from the NRSV.

4. A superb guide to the contemporary scholarship on Hebrews is Daniel J. Harrington, *What Are They Saying about Hebrews?* (New York/Mahwah: Paulist, 2005). See also Richard Ounsworth, "What are They Saying about the Letter to the Hebrews?" *ScriptBull* 39:2 (2009): 76–90. Important recent commentaries include: Harold W. Attridge, *Hebrews*, Hermeneia Series (Philadelphia: Fortress, 1989); Craig R. Koester, *Hebrews*, AB 36 (New York:

essential presuppositions concerning this letter, many of which are shared by a majority of contemporary scholars.

Although the date, authorship, provenance, and destination of Hebrews are contested, many believe it was written sometime between AD 60–100 by an educated, anonymous, Jewish Christian author, who is addressing a community in danger of experiencing the defection of some of its members from the faith (apostasy). Written in elegant Greek (the best in the New Testament), Hebrews has only the loose form of a letter and is best described in its own terms as "a message of encouragement" (13:22, NAB; "word of exhortation," NRSV). Many scholars consider it a sermon or a homily.

Regardless of whether this is the most accurate description of its genre, it is evident that Hebrews exhibits considerable rhetorical refinements that are equally at home in skilled oratory or sermons.[5] It also provides an extraordinary example of the inventive interpretation and reapplication of the Old Testament, typical of highly trained rabbinical practice. While the novel interpretations at times can mystify the modern mind, there can be no doubt of the respect of the author for the Word of God, which indeed is "living and active, sharper than any two-edged sword" and "able to judge the thoughts and intentions of the heart" (4:12). The argument of Hebrews is thoroughly rooted in the Old Testament traditions of Israel, even if occasionally, the author is unclear about the precise location of the source(s) he quotes or

Doubleday, 2001); Alan C. Mitchell, *Hebrews*, ed. Daniel J. Harrington, Sacra Pagina (Collegeville, MN: Liturgical Press, 2007); Thomas G. Long, *Hebrews*, Interpretation Series (Louisville: John Knox, 1997); and James W. Thompson, *Hebrews*, Paideia Series (Grand Rapids: Baker Academic, 2008). Two fine introductions to the theology of Hebrews are Donald A. Hagner, *Encountering the Book of Hebrews: An Exposition* (Grand Rapids: Baker Academic, 2002); and Barnabas Lindars, *The Theology of the Letter to the Hebrews*, New Testament Theology Series (Cambridge: Cambridge University, 1991).

5. Some scholars rightly emphasize that Hebrews was intended to be *heard* rather than read. One could thus properly speak of "hearers" rather than "readers." Centuries later, however, we read this document and call it a "letter." I stick with convention and refer to the author (rather than the "preacher") and designate it a letter.

mentions.[6] He is thus conversant with the traditions of Israel but sees them in a new light, refracted as it were, through a trinitarian[7] and christological prism that brings out new shades of understanding previously hidden.

Yet this highly doctrinal orientation masks a more subtle insight. The author's highly developed theological stance is not done for its own sake. Throughout the letter there are indications that the real reason for this perspective is, in fact, exhortative. As Frank Matera has noted in his excellent *New Testament Theology*, as important as Hebrews' christological perspective is, it is "ultimately at the service of exhortation."[8] The author desires to exhort, to encourage, to strengthen, and to bolster a community being tested, most likely because of persecutions and the temptation to renege on the faith in the face of danger.

Thus in chapter 2 of the letter, when Christ's priestly identity is already stated, his suffering is acknowledged precisely because "he is able to help those who are being tested" (2:18). The letter reinforces this perspective at several points with such exhortations as "Let us hold fast to the confession of our hope without wavering" (10:23). Moreover, the final chapter is also exhortative and is oriented eschatologically toward our heavenly future: "For

---

6. See, for example, the expression "someone has testified somewhere" (2:6; cf. 4:4).

7. Although the Christology of Hebrews overshadows the trinitarian underpinnings, they are nonetheless present. God as "Father" is mentioned only three times, yet the very concept of Jesus as God's Son, which is omnipresent in Hebrews, implies the fatherhood of God. The Holy Spirit is mentioned only seven times in the letter yet functions in accord with both Christian theology in the New Testament and its Old Testament antecedents. A key verse where all three persons of the Trinity are referenced is Hebrews 9:14. For a good exposition of the importance of trinitarian thought for ministry, see Peter Drilling, *Trinity and Ministry* (Minneapolis: Fortress, 1991).

8. Frank J. Matera, *New Testament Theology: Exploring Diversity and Unity* (Louisville: Westminster John Knox, 2007), 336, 349. Similarly, another scholar calls the author of Hebrews "one of the great pastoral theologians of the apostolic period" and describes the letter as "a pastoral theologian's rhetorical effort to shore up the faith" of his community. See John C. Laansma, "Hebrews, Book of," in *Dictionary for Theological Interpretation of the Bible*, ed. Kevin J. Vanhoozer (Grand Rapids: Baker Academic, 2005), 274, 276.

here we have no lasting city, but we are looking for the city that is to come" (13:14). In Hebrews eschatology and exhortation merge to keep the focus on hopeful anticipation as we make our way toward perfection, a prominent theme in Hebrews, following Jesus the High Priest himself.[9] Hebrews can consequently be considered a document of hope, something that Pope Benedict calls attention to with great frequency in his encyclical, *Spe Salvi* (In Hope We Are Saved, 2007).[10]

Although we cannot be more precise about the historical context of the first recipients of this message, we can accept that a proper understanding of Hebrews comes from this context of encouragement.[11] Its doctrinal stance is intended to support those in times of trial. As we shall see, this impacts on our own contemporary understanding of the priesthood as well.

The Principal Message: Jesus Christ, the High Priest

Scholars are generally agreed that the main contribution of this fascinating New Testament book is its unique and highly developed notion of Jesus Christ as the great High Priest (Greek, *archiereus*).[12] This theme, however, is rooted in a more overarching

---

9. The Greek verb *teleioō* ("to complete, be perfect, reach a goal") features prominently in the theology of Hebrews, orienting the hearers/readers to the heavenly Jerusalem where God's salvation will be fully accomplished. The same verb is used of Jesus as "having been made perfect" through his obedience and suffering (Heb 5:9). See John M. Scholer, *Proleptic Priests: Priesthood in the Epistle to the Hebrews*, JSNTSS 49 (Sheffield: Sheffield Academic, 1991), 201–2.

10. The Holy Father uses Hebrews throughout the encyclical, but one of his most striking observations is the strong connection in Hebrews between faith and hope. See *Spe Salvi*, par. 2.

11. There may be a connection with Christians from or in Rome, but no certain judgment can be made (the greetings of "those from Italy," 13:24).

12. Important studies include three works by Albert Vanhoye, *Our Priest is Christ: The Doctrine of the Epistle to the Hebrews* (Rome: Pontifical Biblical Institute, 1977); *Old Testament Priests and the New Priest, according to the New Testament* (Petersham, MA: St. Bede's, 1980); *Structure and Message of the Epistle to the Hebrews*, SubBi 12 (Rome: Pontifical Biblical Institute, 1989); and John M. Scholer's *Proleptic Priests*, mentioned above in n. 9.

christological understanding. Hebrews begins with the announce-
ment of Jesus as the Son of God, a high Christology that shows
Jesus as higher than the angels, divine beings who surround God
and act as his messengers.[13] Jesus is now the messenger "far
superior to the angels" (1:4, NAB). Although Hebrews acknowl-
edges implicitly Jesus' divine Sonship in terms of incarnation, it
is the exaltation after the sacrifice of the cross that is most rele-
vant. His Sonship is intimately connected with his priesthood.[14]
As a faithful Son whose identity comes from his Father, he is
nonetheless made a priest, a man called, set apart, and imbued
with holiness, to make intercession for humankind.[15] Jesus
suffered death, Son though he was, and in doing so was made
perfect through suffering (2:8b-10). He offered himself as the
sacrificial victim. He tasted death for all (2:9b) and was one like
us in everything but sin (4:15). His experience, then, was intimately close to our own, which enabled him to both understand
us and assist us in our struggles. The letter explicitly states:

> Therefore he had to become like his brothers and sisters in
> every respect, so that he might be a merciful and faithful high
> priest in the service of God, to make a sacrifice of atonement
> for the sins of the people. Because he himself was tested by
> what he suffered, he is able to help those who are being tested.
> (2:17-18)

---

13. Actually, Hebrews contains one of only three passages in the New
Testament (Heb 1:8-9; John 1:1; 20:28) that explicitly acclaim Jesus as "God,"
supporting the notion of the letter's high Christology. See Raymond E.
Brown, *Jesus God and Man* (Milwaukee: Bruce, 1967), 23–25.

14. On the nature of Jesus' priesthood as royal, see Deborah W. Rooke,
"Jesus as Royal Priest: Reflections on the Interpretation of the Melchizedek
Tradition in Heb 7," *Bib* 81 (2000): 81–94. Although I am largely persuaded
by Rooke's main thesis that there is a connection between the royal and cultic
identity of Jesus the High Priest, whether it is wise to use the word "onto-
logical" (p. 82) is less certain from a strictly biblical viewpoint. However, it
would be fair to say that Jesus' High Priesthood is not merely *functional* but
is bound up with his identity as God's Son.

15. For the Jewish antecedents of Hebrews' understanding of priesthood,
see Attridge, *Hebrews*, 97–103.

This is the first comprehensive statement about Jesus the High Priest in Hebrews, and it both concludes a section devoted to exhortation and the example of Jesus' self-abasement and subsequent exaltation, and begins setting forth an extensive exploration of this High Priest who is in every way superior to what had come before (Heb 3–10).

Jesus the High Priest

Since the design of the letter is quite complex and our scope and time are limited, I will summarize as succinctly as possible the high priestly theology of Hebrews.[16] Hebrews begins with the assertion that Jesus, as God's faithful and obedient Son, is superior to Moses, the faithful lawgiver and servant of God (3:1-6). When he describes Jesus' priesthood (4:14–5:10), it is in these terms.

- He exercises his ministry from heaven, where he has already passed to exaltation and sits at God's right hand (4:14; also 1:3, 13; 8:1; 10:12; 12:2).[17]

- He sympathizes with our weaknesses because he is exactly like us, having been taken from among human beings, but without sin (4:15; 5:1).

- He has not chosen his own identity but was called by God and sent on mission (5:4; 3:1).

- Just as the High Priest of old entered the Holy of Holies on the Day of Atonement and offered sacrifices for the sins of the people (9:7), so Jesus Christ has entered a heavenly

---

16. For background on the biblical vocabulary of priesthood (Hebrew, *kōhēn*; Greek, *hiereus* and *archeireus*) see *TDOT* VII.60–75; *TDNT* III.257–83; *EDNT* 2.174. A good overview of the Old Testament priesthood can be found in Merlin D. Rehm, "Levites and Priests," *ABD* 4.297–310.

17. Sitting at God's right hand (1:3, 13; 8:1; 10:12; 12:2) is not meant to indicate a mode of rest but a position of power and authority; it constitutes a location whence Jesus still acts as High Priest. See David R. Anderson, *The King-Priest of Psalm 110 in Hebrews*, SBL 21 (New York: Peter Lang, 2001), 174.

sanctuary, having offered sacrifices for sin, offering himself as victim (5:1; 9:12, 14, 25; 10:10).

• He learned obedience through suffering (5:8).

• His sufferings made him "perfect" and the source of salvation, redemption, purification, forgiveness, sanctification, and perfection for all (5:9; 10:18, 22).

• As High Priest chosen and exalted by God his Father he is our forerunner (Greek, *prodomos*, 6:20).

• His royal priesthood has made him mediator of a new and better covenant (7:22; 8:6, 13; 12:24).[18]

• In essence, Jesus' priesthood both fulfills and yet exceeds and abolishes the Old Testament cult in favor of a new cult (7:18; 8:13-14; 9:14; 10:9).

This is an impressive and comprehensive view of Jesus' priesthood.

The Figure of Melchizedek

Melchizedek's role in this scenario is crucial. Jesus' royal priestly identity is not bound to Israel's historical priesthood, which was tied to the figure of Aaron and the tribe of Levi, which God set apart for priestly service. Unlike the Levitical priesthood, which was passed on through generations by family lines and tribal identity, Jesus' priestly identity is traced to the mysterious figure of Melchizedek by way of Psalm 110:4, which features prominently in the author's exposition: "You are a priest forever according to the order of Melchizedek" (Heb 5:6, 10; 6:20; 7:17, 21).[19]

---

18. Covenant theology is prominent in Hebrews. At times, however, there is a play on the word covenant (Greek, *diathēkē*), which can also mean "last will and testament" (9:17; cf. 9:15).

19. In an extensive study of Psalm 110 in Hebrews, one scholar suggests that Hebrews 5:1-10, in particular, makes a unique contribution to the theology of the High Priesthood of Jesus Christ by explicitly connecting Ps 2:7

Melchizedek is an obscure and mysterious figure about whom little is known (Gen 14:22). He is said to be "King of Salem" (likely, Jerusalem) and "priest of God Most High" (Heb 7:1) who blessed Abraham (Abram) and brought out bread and wine for him after Abraham defeated certain kings and rescued his nephew Lot (Gen 14:17-20). Abraham, in turn, rewarded Melchizedek with a tenth of his goods. Melchizedek's association with Abraham, the ancestor of Aaron and the Levi, the source of Israel's inherited priesthood, gives him chronological and honorific precedence. As with so many characters in the Bible, Melchizedek suddenly appears on stage for his cameo performance and just as suddenly disappears offstage. The author of Hebrews, however, draws attention to this brief appearance and makes the most of it:

> His name, in the first place, means "king of righteousness"; next he is also king of Salem, that is, "king of peace." Without father, without mother, without genealogy, having neither beginning of days nor end of life, but resembling the Son of God, he remains a priest forever. (Heb 7:2-3)

Melchizedek is consequently the perfect foreshadowing of Jesus' unique identity. This elusive figure provides several essential elements to Hebrews' Christology, in particular: divine rather than human origins, a royal and priestly identity not tied to human lineage yet fully human, and high priestly status that mediates cultically between God and humanity and provides blessing, hospitality (bread and wine), and peace (Hebrew, *shalom*). What is left unsaid but perhaps can be presupposed in the background is that the high priest in Israel, by virtue of his breastplate containing the names of the twelve tribes, was representative of the whole people. Hebrews clearly envisions Jesus as possessing a universal role for his people as High Priest. His once for all

---

and Ps 110:4. See Anderson, *The King-Priest*, 288. With many commentators, Anderson also points to the chiastic parallel in 5:1-10 in which vv. 5-6, the Old Testament quotations, are central. See also Lindars, *Theology of the Letter to the Hebrews*, 61, and Scholer, *Proleptic Priests*, 87.

sacrifice of his own body (7:27; 10:10) continues to intercede for his people from his heavenly throne (7:25).

In this theology of the High Priesthood of Jesus Christ, Hebrews holds together certain elements that should in normal parlance be seen in tension. Jesus is both priest and victim. He is both the one who offers the sacrifice and the sacrifice being offered. He is both fully human in his identity, especially in his ability to identify with our human state, and yet he is exalted above even the angels and is enthroned forever in a heavenly sanctuary. His sacrifice was made once for all, yet his intercession on behalf of his own people never ceases. We have already received the salvation and redemption achieved by this sacrifice, yet there is more to come in the eschatological age. He is made perfect, yet perfection for his people remains a future goal and an undimmed hope. Jesus' high priestly ministry both fulfills and annuls the old cult. In these tensions perhaps we could say that Hebrews is eminently a "catholic" writing in its ability to embrace the "both/and" dimensions of life.[20] They are not contradictory, but they remain in tension.

It is also interesting to see what is left out of this scenario. Curiously, Hebrews never picks up on the image of bread and wine associated with Melchizedek. The eucharistic overtones of this imagery are unmistakable. Many scholars conclude that Hebrews does not mention the eucharist at all, though some experts take the phrase "sacrifice of praise" (13:15) as an allusion to the sacra-

---

20. Hebrews is perhaps the most obvious New Testament document that could, if not carefully interpreted, lead to supersessionism (negating the value of the Old Testament and its religion in favor of the New). This is a danger to be avoided. Hebrews is not really supersessionist, in part because of this dual tendency to accept "both/and" tensions, and because the Old Testament foundations are critically necessary to understand the letter's unique theological perspective. All the major details associated with the High Priesthood of Jesus are from the Old Testament. The author is more in line with the Matthean Jesus, who speaks of fulfilling, not abolishing, the law (Matt 5:17). More cautiously, Andrew Lincoln warns against jettisoning the notion of supersessionism altogether, as both Judaism and Christianity have succumbed to it at one time or another (e.g., the sacrificial system of the temple). See his *Hebrews: A Guide* (London: T&T Clark, 2006), 118.

ment.[21] Another notable lack is the use of shepherding imagery, which we have come to associate strongly with ordained ministry. Only near the end of the letter is Jesus called the "great shepherd of the sheep," in the only passage that also mentions explicitly the resurrection (13:20). But unlike in John's gospel, the image is not developed.

One also notes that two of the three traditional "powers" of the priesthood (Latin, *munera*)—teaching (*munus docendi*), divine worship (*munus liturgicum*), governing (*munus regendi*)—are not developed to any great degree.[22] The prominence of the high priesthood imagery overshadows the royal and teaching (prophetic) dimensions of the priesthood of Jesus Christ in favor of the cultic, sacrificial office. The seeds of these latter two offices of the priesthood are present, but they remain in the background.

Since an argument from silence is always tenuous, we should not draw too many conclusions from these anomalies, other than to say that they do not feature prominently in the Christology of Hebrews. The focus remains nonetheless on the High Priesthood of Jesus Christ, the exalted Lord, the Son of God.

This unique New Testament teaching is as broad as it is deep. While maintaining continuity with the Old Testament traditions of the priesthood, Hebrews embarks on its own novel path to breathtaking christological innovation.

The Influence of Hebrews in the Church's Theology of Priesthood

One cannot exaggerate the influence of the Letter to the Hebrews on the Catholic Church's theology of the priesthood. From its liturgical rites of ordination to its catechism and to official documents on the priesthood, the church has utilized the

21. Lindars, *Theology of the Letter to the Hebrews*, 139. He adds, however, that the understanding of the Eucharist as sacrifice did not arise until after the New Testament period, beginning with the *Didache*.
22. CCC par. 1592; *PDV* par. 26. The royal dimension can be seen in the figure of Melchizedek himself, a king, and the prophetic or teaching dimension is seen both in Jesus' connection to the Word of God (Heb 1:2-3; 6:5) and the mention of the leaders' faithful rendering of it (Heb 13:7).

theology of Hebrews to great effect, explicitly and implicitly.[23] We should note, however, a striking truth. In the development of its theology of the priesthood, the church has gone where Hebrews itself never went. Nowhere in Hebrews (or in the New Testament) is there an application of the High Priesthood of Jesus Christ to the ministerial priesthood! Indeed, when leaders in the community are mentioned in Hebrews, the terminology used is much vaguer. They are called leaders (Greek, *hēgoumenoi* [13:7, 17, 24]) and no description of their duties is given. They are not called priests, a term that in the New Testament is never applied to Christian leaders but only to Old Testament figures, Jesus being the sole exception.[24] As Albert Vanhoye summarizes:

> By its imposing volume, the priestly christology of the Epistle to the Hebrews brings out very clearly the most important point of the Christian position in regard to the priesthood: there is only one priest in the full sense of the term and this priest is Christ. Christ alone has been able [to] fulfill effectively the essential function of the priesthood, which is to establish a mediation between God and mankind [*sic*]. He is the sole mediator. . . . A single new priest therefore succeeds to the multitude of Old Testament priests.[25]

This is the most profound teaching of Hebrews. Priests are by definition intermediaries between God and humanity, the spiritual and the secular. They are by nature called to a special holiness, set apart for service, which allows them to perform their

---

23. In my own Sulpician spiritual tradition, which is rooted in the seventeenth-century French school of spirituality, Hebrews was the main source for a high theology of the priesthood. One author goes so far as to say that Hebrews contains the entire doctrinal content of the French school's teaching. So, Eugene A. Walsh, *The Priesthood in the Writings of the French School: Bérulle, De Condren, Olier*, STD thesis (Washington: Catholic University of America, 1949), 24.

24. Hebrews also twice labels Jesus a "leader" (NAB) but with a different word (Greek, *archēgos* [2:10; 12:2]), which has the nuance of an innovative leader or "pioneer," the translation used in the NRSV.

25. Vanhoye, *Old Testament Priests*, 312–13. Note how the very title of his book makes his point clear.

cultic rites, their sacral duties, as intermediaries. They are sup-
posed to be avenues to the divine. Whereas in the past there were
priests (plural) to take on this role, now in Jesus Christ there is
but one priest, the great High Priest who as God's Son fulfills
this role perfectly. He established free access to God for all in a
way only a faithful Son could do by self-sacrifice to his Father's
will. Albert Vanhoye's words again hit the mark:

> Christ is not a member of a priestly family and on his cross he
> is far from fulfilling the requirements of ritual purity! If access
> to the sanctuary was formerly reserved to the high priest
> alone, now, on the contrary, all are invited to go forward with
> assurance by the way Christ opened up with his own blood
> (10:19-20).[26]

This special priesthood cannot be copied. It is permanent and it
is uniquely tied to the person of Christ, the only New Testament
priest.

Yet, for valid reasons and—from a faith perspective—under
the guidance of the Holy Spirit in the ongoing development of
theology, the church came to apply much of the terminology in
Hebrews tied to Christ's identity as High Priest to the ministerial
priesthood by way of *analogy*. The priesthood today, or originally
the "presbyterate" (from Greek *presbyteros*, "elder"), is but an
analogous participation in the one priesthood of Jesus Christ.[27]
We will now briefly examine some of the church's teaching in
two of its most important documents on the priesthood, *Presbyterorum Ordinis* (*PO*), Vatican Council II's "Decree on Priestly
Ministry and Life" (1965), and *Pastores Dabo Vobis* (*PDV*), Pope

---

26. Vanhoye, *Our Priest is Christ*, 42.
27. It is also worth noting that Hebrews does not apply priestly terminology to the people of God. We must look elsewhere in the New Testament
for an understanding of "the priesthood of the faithful" (1 Pet 2:5; Rev 1:6;
5:10; 20:6). This concept, though, is also properly rooted in an Old Testament
tradition of a priestly people, the holy nation of Israel (Exod 19:6). See *LG*
par. 10.

John Paul II's postsynodal "Apostolic Exhortation on Priestly Formation" (1992).[28]

Vatican II's Decree on Priestly Ministry and Life

The most obvious message of the application of Hebrews in *Presbyterorum Ordinis* is that the ministerial priesthood is modeled entirely after the priesthood of Jesus Christ. The document cites or quotes Hebrews explicitly some eleven times. Using the letter as its inspiration, what is striking is the direct and immediate application that is made to the ministerial priesthood. *Presbyterorum Ordinis* makes the following main points:

- Priests live on earth but mediate heavenly matters, by offering gifts and sacrifices for sins; they are chosen from among human beings yet remain their brothers (*PO* par. 3; Heb 5:1).

- Our priesthood is an imitation of Christ's (*PO* par. 3; Heb 2:17; 4:15).

- Like Christ, priests should exercise hospitality, kindness, and sharing of possessions (*PO* par. 8; Heb 13:1-2, 16).

- The priesthood is a universal service, valid for all peoples at all times (*PO* par. 10; Heb 7:3).

- Christ's own holiness as the great High Priest makes up for the lack of holiness on the part of priests (*PO* par. 12; Heb 7:26).

---

28. Both documents are available in English in various editions. I have used an electronic version on CD titled *Church Documents*, 8th ed. (Boston: Pauline Books & Media, 2002). Vatican II's Dogmatic Constitution on the Church (*Lumen Gentium*) also contains a section on the priesthood (par. 28) that dovetails with *Presbyterorum Ordinis*. Another official document that incorporates some insights from these works was issued by the Congregation for Clergy, *Directory for the Ministry and Life of Priests* (Vatican: Libreria Editrice Vaticana, 1994). Interestingly, Vatican II's Decree on the Training of Priests (*Optatam Totius*, 1965) does not mention Hebrews at all. *Pastores Dabo Vobis* makes up for this lacuna.

- Priests are called to enter God's sanctuary with sincere hearts, put the Word of God in practice, and share the wisdom of God (*PO* par. 13; Heb 10:19, 22; 13:9-10).

- Priests should be men of faith, just as Abraham was a model of faith (*PO* par. 22; Heb 11:8).

This use of Hebrews obviously does not provide a total theology of the priesthood, but we should note its fidelity to the spirit of Hebrews, especially in the balance between the humanity of the priests and their sacral duties. Jesus Christ is the model; he is the one who provides the sanctity we ourselves can never provide.

John Paul II's Apostolic Exhortation on Priestly Formation

Pastores Dabo Vobis quotes or alludes to Hebrews more than a dozen times. Its pastoral orientation, however, comes across even more quickly than in *Presbyterorum Ordinis*. In the opening paragraphs, *Pastores Dabo Vobis* immediately connects the title in Hebrews of Christ, "the great shepherd of the sheep" (13:20), to God's promise recorded in Jeremiah to give shepherds for the flock (Jer 3:15; 23:4) and to the image of the "Good Shepherd" from John's gospel (John 10:11; cf. 21:15-19).[29] Like *Presbyterorum Ordinis*, this document also emphasizes the human dimension of the ministerial priesthood, and it does so utilizing two quotations from Hebrews (5:1; 4:15), stating explicitly at the beginning of chapter one: "The Letter to the Hebrews clearly affirms the 'human character' of God's minister."[30]

This is a significant indicator of the document's pastoral character, I believe, because *Pastores Dabo Vobis* is the first official

---

29. *PDV* par. 1. The opening quotation from Jeremiah (in the Latin Vulgate) provides the document's title, "I will give you shepherds." Most theologians consider *Pastores Dabo Vobis* to be the most important official teaching on the priesthood since Vatican II. It was the result of the 1990 synod of bishops on priestly formation, and its teaching has directed the model of priestly formation adopted in many countries, especially in the United States. See the U.S. bishops' *Program of Priestly Formation*, 5th ed. (Washington: USCCB, 2006).

30. *PDV* par. 5.

teaching of the church to emphasize human formation as one of the four main pillars of priestly formation and, in fact, as foundational to forming good priests.[31] There is no question that Jesus is the model, for the text of the apostolic exhortation says: "The priest, who is called to be a 'living image' of Jesus Christ, head and shepherd of the church, should seek to reflect in himself, as far as possible, the human perfection which shines forth in the incarnate Son of God."[32] This orientation in *Pastores Dabo Vobis* is quite remarkable, not only for its emphasis on the human qualities needed for priestly ministry,[33] but also for its fidelity to Hebrews, which in fact blends well the human and divine aspects of the ministry of Jesus the High Priest.

In addition to this basic stance, *Pastores Dabo Vobis* also applies Hebrews quite directly to the ministerial priesthood in three other important ways:

- Ministerial priests are configured to Christ, shepherd and head of the church, and participate in mediating the direct access to God Christ has achieved as High Priest; Christ fulfilled the Old Testament roles of mediation previously performed by kings, priests and prophets; ministerial priests now share this threefold ministry (*PDV* par. 13; Heb 8–9; esp. 9:24-28).

- Priestly vocation is a mysterious call by God's grace; it must be answered with full freedom; Christ makes up for our weaknesses even as we are called to perfection (*PDV* par. 20; Heb 7:26).

- Christ is the definitive Word of God; priests should be formed well to communicate faithfully the true wisdom of God (*PDV* par. 53; Heb 1:1-4).

---

31. *PDV* par. 43, which cites Heb 5:1 a second time. The other three pillars are spiritual, intellectual, and pastoral formation.

32. *PDV* par. 43.

33. See also *PDV* par. 47 and 72 where Hebrews (2:17; 4:15) is referred to twice more in the context of the human qualities necessary for priests.

While these statements are consistent with the teaching of Vatican II, much of which is quoted or referenced in the apostolic exhortation, it is noteworthy that *Pastores Dabo Vobis* develops much more thoroughly a theology of the priesthood that puts flesh on the bones of the council's teaching. It provides a far more extensive understanding. While it is replete with doctrinal insight, its pastoral sensitivity is equally apparent, a style that blends well with the character of Hebrews.[34]

Pastoral Applications

Having looked at Hebrews itself and the two principal church documents on the priesthood, we now turn to our own pressing pastoral question. What lessons can be learned from the Letter to the Hebrews that can be applied to Catholic priests today? I point to six principal teachings that I think are particularly pertinent to our contemporary situation.

The Unwavering Focus on Jesus Christ

First and foremost, the unmistakable focus on Jesus is preeminent in Hebrews. The call to perseverance in the faith is accompanied by the invitation to keep our eyes fixed on Jesus, "the pioneer and perfecter of our faith" (12:2). Nothing could be more important today in the life of priests. Not only is Jesus our model for the priesthood and its perfect embodiment, but in a contemporary yet traditional theology of the priest as "another Christ" (Latin, *alter Christus*), Hebrews is all the more important.

Priesthood is all about Christ. He is the only real priest. We priests act *in persona Christi Capitis* (in the person of Christ the head [of the church]) but really it is Christ who acts in us (Gal 2:20).[35] We are not literally but sacramentally other Christs. Thomas Aquinas said it best: "Christ is the source of all priesthood: the priest of the old law was a figure of Christ, and the

---

34. A succinct summation of these teachings, as well as many others from church history, can be found in the *Catechism of the Catholic Church* (CCC par. 1539–53).

35. CCC par. 1548.

priest of the new law acts in the person of Christ."[36] The expectation that priests should represent Christ concretely in people's lives is not merely pious theology. It is rightly intended to be a way of *being* and not merely a way of *doing*. We are given a share in the sacred power (*sacra potestas*) of Christ the High Priest.[37] It is ultimately a call to integrity and authenticity to the mysterious call of our priestly vocation, to be conformed perfectly to Christ who molds us, shapes us, and gives us our very being. But we must also remember, although it is not Hebrews that speaks to the issue, that our priesthood is not the only type given to the church. Vatican II strongly reminds us of the priesthood of the faithful, rooted in other New Testament documents, which also should profoundly shape our own living out of the ministerial priesthood we have received.[38]

Given the high Christology and theology of Hebrews, we priests especially could well reflect upon how we can better incarnate this modeling of Christ as we go about our ministries.

A Unique Priesthood, Source of a Vocation

A second application stems from the unique emphasis on the kind of priesthood Jesus had. Unlike the priests of the Old Testament, it was not hereditary. It was not automatic because one was born to it. It was rooted in the mysterious call of his Father, in the mold of Melchizedek who had no lineage but was a chosen king and priest. Our theology of priesthood rightfully emphasizes the mystery of a vocation.[39] It is a call, not self-chosen but a call to which we respond.[40] Interestingly, the only place Jesus is called an "apostle" is in Hebrews (3:1). He shares with us a divine call that he received from his Father and a divine mission that he accepted. Jesus was sent on mission from his Father. Priests, in turn, are called and sent by him on mission. Our identity and our ministry are bound up with the mystery of God at

---

36. *Summa Theologiae* III, 22, 4c, quoted in *CCC* par. 1548.
37. *CCC* par. 1538.
38. *LG* par. 10; *CCC* par. 1539.
39. *PDV* par. 34, 36.
40. *PDV* par. 36, which draws attention to Jesus' words in John 15:16.

work through human resources, calling ministerial priests into being. This mystery of the vocation is not entirely in our control, but it gets tested and requires discipline, both of which Jesus experienced.

The Balance between Human and Divine

A third lesson concerns the balance between the human and divine, the sacred and profane, that one finds in Hebrews. On the one hand, as we have noted, it has one of the highest Christologies of the New Testament. In its understanding of Christ the High Priest, it exalts him in a way far above any human aspirations. On the other hand, the letter insists that even Christ was like us in all things but sin. Even this High Priest, unique Son of God that he is, is chosen from among men and can identify with our frailties, our sufferings, our limitations. Priests are at one and the same time called to a particular holiness (not higher!),[41] while acknowledging our human limitations. While we can never perfectly imitate Jesus as High Priest, we can try to integrate better the human and divine aspects of our ministry. Even while we proclaim the Gospel message to others, we remain conscious that we ourselves are not the "masters" of the Word, but its servants.[42] Even while we dispense the sacraments and mediate God's grace to others, we are mindful that we ourselves need to receive the same divine aid and be touched by the same healing power of God.[43] This dynamic tension between the human and divine in the ministerial priesthood is ever-present.

Priests as Pastoral Theologians

Fourth, Hebrews can teach us about the wisdom of being "pastoral theologians," for that is what I think the author was, and that is what we are called to be. The subtle blending in Hebrews of profound doctrinal depth, and sublime theological understanding about Jesus Christ himself, served to inspire, encourage, strengthen, and challenge the people for whom the message was

41. *Pastores Dabo Vobis* (par. 17) is quite explicit about this point.
42. *PDV* par. 26.
43. *PDV* par. 26.

first written. It does the same for us. Hebrews reminds us of a truth about the priesthood emphasized in Vatican II and reinforced in *Pastores Dabo Vobis*, namely, the intimate connection between our own priestly identity and spirituality and the people we serve. *Pastores Dabo Vobis* calls it "an intimate bond that exists between the priest's spiritual life and the exercise of his ministry."[44] As I read Hebrews, I believe one sees evidence of this bond. The deep and wise reflection on the ministry of Jesus the High Priest helped the author to reinterpret the Old Testament traditions in a way that also nourished his threatened community. We should not be reticent to put our theological insights to work as we seek to become more effective pastoral theologians.

Eschatological Perspective

A fifth teaching in Hebrews stems from its eschatological orientation and the context of trial and tribulation that is an undercurrent in the letter. The theology of Hebrews, profound as it is, was not developed for its own sake by a systematic theologian. It was pronounced as a message of encouragement to a community under stress, fraught with the danger of apostasy in light of impending persecution or severe trials. It also strives to exhort the faithful to remain steady in their stance of faith as they journey toward perfection. The goal is the heavenly Jerusalem (12:22). As with all eschatologically oriented documents, Hebrews is intended to impart hope to its hearers/readers. The message obviously is phrased in various ways but always with a combination of challenge and encouragement:

- Just as Jesus was tested in suffering, so he can identify with us when we undergo the same (2:18).

- Because we have this secure High Priest who has already accomplished our salvation, "Let us hold fast to the confession of our hope without wavering, for he who has promised is faithful" (10:23).

---

44. *PDV* par. 24, cf. also *PO* par. 12.

- "Endure trials for the sake of discipline" (12:7).

- "Strengthen your drooping hands and your weak knees" (12:12, NAB).

Given what the priesthood and the church has endured in recent years, we can properly see ourselves as a people in need of such advice, as we, too, journey toward perfection. As Pope Benedict XVI has reminded us in his encyclical, *Spe Salvi,* hope and faith go together intimately and, along with the virtue of love, sustain the life of the church on our pilgrim journey.

Priest as "Victim"

Sixth and finally, just as Jesus was both priest and victim, priests today should reflect on the radical nature of our call to serve others. This message, of course, is rooted in Jesus of Nazareth's own teaching that he came to serve and not to be served (Matt 20:26-28; Mark 10:43-45). But for Hebrews, Jesus as victim is tied to his offering of his blood and his flesh, his sacrifice on the cross, and his subsequent vindication in the resurrection and exaltation at God's right hand.

We priests today, naturally, do not make the same sacrifice, even though we make it present through the power of the Holy Spirit in the celebration of the Eucharist daily.[45] But analogously, we are called to self-abnegation, surrender to the will of the Father, and to follow the call of discipleship even though it may lead to suffering. We need to become, metaphorically speaking, "victims" in the sense of surrender to the Father's will. I see two equally important sides to this expectation, outward and inward. Outwardly, a priest's participation in the suffering of Jesus the High Priest should help us identify and empathize with those who suffer, just as his experience enabled him to be one with humanity in our trials and tribulations. Inwardly, priests are called to enter into the passion of Christ the High Priest by our acceptance and endurance of the difficulties and the suffering

---

45. CCC par. 1545.

that comes our way. Both means incarnate the practice of Christ the High Priest.

Sadly, the language of high priesthood (*alter Christus*, etc.) and the exalted nature of priesthood sometimes lead to entitlement rather than selfless service. Some priests seemingly lack the capacity for true empathy with those who suffer. Others, when things are simply not going their way or they meet great challenges in pastoral ministry, give up, lose hope, or walk away. Even worse, perhaps, is falling into the trap of clericalism, which is a distortion of the true priesthood. Priests sometimes begin to see themselves as the privileged class, and there are always people willing to put us on a pedestal. This is a corruption of the call to priesthood in the mold of the High Priest, Jesus Christ. It is an inherent danger in a high theology of priesthood. But, in my judgment, Hebrews maintains the balance. Priesthood is about ministry, serving others in the person of Christ. It is simultaneously a humbling and an exhilarating experience.

Conclusion

This "fascinating and unsettling" book beckons us in the third Christian millennium to examine carefully where we have come from and where we need to go as church and as priests of God.[46] This New Testament letter, the only document from its unknown author and the only source of our theology of Christ the High Priest, does not give us every aspect of priesthood or ministry as our understanding has developed through the ages. There are other dimensions covered by different New Testament perspectives, such as the shepherding imagery from the Johannine literature, the threefold hierarchical ministries (bishop, priest, deacon) that evolved from the Pastoral Epistles, the spousal imagery that comes from the Pauline tradition, the practice of celibacy or the call to simplicity of life that come from the teaching and example of Jesus, more developed thought on Jesus as Prophet and King, and so on.

---

46. This apt description comes from Laansma, "Hebrews," 280.

Yet one can scarcely imagine understanding the priesthood without Hebrews. As Albert Vahoye says, "The more we meditate on the Epistle to the Hebrews the more we are awestruck by the riches which it offers us."[47] It places our whole understanding on a firm foundation, the person of Jesus Christ himself. We should glory in this fact. And it is entirely appropriate that we reflect in awe, during this year for priests, on the great gift that the priesthood is for the church and for the world.

While it is a time to support the priesthood and priests and to give thanks to God for priestly service, it is not a time to make of priests something we are not. If we are "other Christs," it is only as pale reflections of the real Priest. As members of the same pilgrim church, we journey with all the faithful, who share in the same priesthood of Jesus Christ albeit in a different way,[48] toward that heavenly Jerusalem to which Jesus beckons us. This is, however, a time to renew ourselves in the one priesthood of Jesus Christ. Let us heed the words of Hebrews itself:

> Remember your leaders, those who spoke the word of God to you; consider the outcome of their way of life, and imitate their faith. Jesus Christ is the same yesterday and today and forever. (Heb 13:7-8)

47. Vanhoye, *Structure and Message*, 73.
48. CCC par. 1539.

Chapter 2

Living Sacraments:
Some Reflections on Priesthood in Light of the French School and Documents of the Magisterium

Very Rev. Lawrence B. Terrien, SS

In speaking about evolutions in the theology of priesthood since the Second Vatican Council, I have often cited an article by Jesuit Father Peter Fink that appeared in *America Magazine* in 1981.[1] I have always thought that this brief article marked a turning point in American thought on the question. Fink argues that too much of the theological literature up to that point took one or another of the functions of priesthood—the celebration of the sacraments, the proclamation of the Word, or pastoral care—as the starting point for articulating a vision of ordained ministry. He says that these approaches are in the end too limited and limiting. They can only give us a priest who is a functionary. He seeks to rehabilitate a more profound sacramental foundation for our theology of orders, rooted in a renewed understanding of sacraments. In his presentation, the priest by his ordination becomes a sacramental figure himself, a sign of the priestliness of the church as a whole. In this vision, the priesthood of the ordained is indeed ordered to the priesthood of the faithful and is intended to foster and promote this priestliness in the larger

---

1. Peter Fink, "The Other Side of Priesthood," *America*, April 11, 1981.

sense rather than replace it. I believe that most of the theological literature that has appeared in the last twenty-five years moves precisely in the direction of reinforcing the sacramental vision of ordained ministry.[2]

This is certainly confirmed in the postsynodal document on priestly formation. According to *Pastores Dabo Vobis*, the priest, by his ordination, is configured to Christ the Head, Shepherd, and Spouse of the church. He becomes a sign of the continuing presence of Christ who, as the one and only High Priest, the unique leader and guide of the community of his disciples, uses human instruments to carry on his ministry. Those who are ordained do not replace him but render him present. They act, especially in the sacraments, *in persona Christi*. They speak his words of consecration in the first person; pronounce forgiveness in his name and by his authority. However, it may also be said that every act of the ministry is, or should be, in some measure a prolongation of his work in the world.

The Theology and Spirituality of Priesthood in *Pastores Dabo Vobis*

Pastores Dabo Vobis divides its discussion of priestly identity into three sections, beginning with a trinitarian foundation (par. 12), proceeding to a reflection on the priest's configuration to Christ the Head of the church (par. 13–15), and concluding with the mission of service to the church and the world (par. 16–18).

The Source of Priestly Identity in the Trinity

Rooting priestly identity in the Trinity is one of the most interesting theological contributions of this document, because it builds into the very structure of priesthood an essentially

2. Cf. among other works cited in this article: Kenan Osborne: *Priesthood: A History of the Ordained Ministry in the Roman Catholic Church* (New York: Paulist Press, 1988); Avery Dulles, *The Priestly Office: A Theological Reflection* (New York: Paulist Press, 1997); Walter Kasper, *Leadership in the Church* (New York: Herder and Herder, 2003).

relational element as well as a strong sense of mission.[3] In *Trinity and Ministry* Peter Drilling argues that a trinitarian approach to all ministry in the church provides a solid base for differentiating roles without compromising the fundamental equality and dignity of all those incorporated into Christ by baptism. Moreover, the notion of *perichoresis* in trinitarian theology, whereby all of the persons of the Trinity are present and active in all the external works of God because of the constant mutual exchange of life and love within the Trinity, reinforces an essentially collegial structure to ordained ministry and an interactive structure for all ministry in the church.[4] Ordained ministry and all ministerial service are seen as extensions of the mission of the Son and Spirit in the world. Accordingly, ordained ministry must be defined with both christological and pneumatological dimensions, and *Pastores Dabo Vobis* develops these elements in treating configuration to Christ the Head as well as the relationship between the ordained priesthood and the priesthood of all the faithful.

The Configuration to Christ the Head and Shepherd

The notion of *alter Christus,* so strongly associated with ordained priesthood since the Council of Trent, has virtually disappeared from discussions of priesthood since the Second Vatican Council. Robert Schwartz argued in his *Servant Leaders of the People of God* that this expression should be allowed to disappear; he contends

---

3. Cf. *Pastores Dabo Vobis,* par. 12: "Indeed, the priest, by virtue of the consecration which he receives in the Sacrament of Orders, is sent forth by the Father through the mediatorship of Jesus Christ, to whom he is configured in a special way as Head and Shepherd of his people, in order to live and work by the power of the Holy Spirit in service of the Church and for the salvation of the world. In this way the fundamentally 'relational' dimension of priestly identity can be understood. Through the priesthood which arises from the depths of the ineffable mystery of God, that is, from the love of the Father, the grace of Jesus Christ and the Holy Spirit's gift of unity, the priest sacramentally enters into communion with the Bishop and with other priests, in order to serve the People of God who are the Church and to draw all mankind to Christ in accordance with the Lord's prayer."

4. Cf. Peter Drilling, *Trinity and Ministry* (Minneapolis: Fortress Press, 1991), pp. 33–42 for the implications of this approach.

that it compromises the one priesthood of Christ.[5] Nonetheless, the priest is called to represent Christ in and to the community.[6] And perhaps the expression can be rehabilitated. May this not be what is common to all priesthood, that of the ordained as well as the royal priesthood of all believers? Everyone is called to put on Christ, to be another Christ present and active in service to the world for the sake of its transformation and salvation. If so, however, then genuine differentiation of roles needs further specification. The notion of configuration of the ordained to Christ the Head and Shepherd provides such a specification. When *Pastores Dabo Vobis* speaks of the configuration to Christ the Head, it begins with a reflection on the priesthood of Christ that is described in terms of the paschal mystery and that includes the priesthood of all:

> With the one definitive sacrifice of the Cross, Jesus communicated to all his disciples the dignity and mission of priests of the new and eternal Covenant. . . . The new priestly people which is the Church not only has its authentic image in Christ, but also receives from him a real ontological share in his one eternal priesthood, to which she must conform every aspect of her life. (par. 13)

The document goes on to explain that it was "for the sake of this universal priesthood" that Jesus gathered disciples and appointed the Twelve. These were given a particular share in Jesus' own mission and entrusted with special authority for the evangelization of the world and the building up of the church. The gift of the Spirit was given to them so that they might continue his mission. The Twelve in turn called others to assist in this work. It is by virtue of their configuration to Christ the Head by

---

5. Cf. Robert Schwartz, *Servant Leaders of the People of God* (New York: Paulist Press, 1989), pp. 195–96.

6. Cf. e.g., Avery Dulles, "Models of Ministerial Priesthood, *Origins* 20 (1990), pp. 284–89, p. 288: "As in the case of the disciples sent out on mission, Christ gives his priests authority to represent him—to speak and act in his name."

the same Spirit in the sacrament of orders that these others then exercise their various duties:

> In the Church and on behalf of the Church, priests are a sacramental representation of Jesus Christ, the Head and Shepherd, authoritatively proclaiming his Word, repeating his acts of forgiveness and his offer of salvation, particularly in Baptism, Penance and the Eucharist, showing his loving concern to the point of a total gift of self for the flock, which they gather into unity and lead to the Father through Christ and in the Spirit. In a word, priests exist and act in order to proclaim the Gospel to the world and to build up the Church in the name of Christ the Head and Shepherd. (par. 15)

There are two particularly interesting features to this section of the document. First, the priesthood of the ordained is "ordered" to the priesthood of the faithful; the establishment of a specialized ministry was "for the sake of" the priesthood of all.[7] Second, the description of Christ's headship in terms of self-sacrifice and service provides a focus for the spirituality of the priesthood that the document will stress strongly in the third chapter.[8]

---

7. Cf. par. 16: "The ministry of the priest is entirely on behalf of the Church; it aims at promoting the exercise of the common priesthood of the entire people of God." There is a tension between this statement and the passage from par. 15 cited immediately above. Par. 15 seems to give priority to proclaiming the gospel to the world and this paragraph to serving the faith community. This tension is never resolved; nor should we expect to see it resolved. The ministerial tension between mission efforts and service of settled communities is as old as the New Testament.

8. With so much emphasis on the priest as representative of Christ, standing in the forefront of the church, a statement like this is a necessary balance. Otherwise, there is a risk of putting the priest back on a pedestal (although recent events such as the scandal of sexual abuse by priests renders such a development unlikely). The reference in par. 20 to Augustine (*Sermo* 340) reinforces both this identification and the differentiation of roles: "For you I am a Bishop, with you I am a Christian. . . . If therefore it is to me a greater cause for joy to have been rescued with you than to have been placed as your leader, following the Lord's command, I will devote myself to the best of my abilities to serve you, so as not to show myself ungrateful to him who rescued me with that price which has made me your fellow servant."

In Service to the Church and the World

The third section of the discussion of priestly identity presents the priesthood in its relationships to the church and to the world.

> If the priest's most fundamental relationship is to Jesus Christ, Head and Shepherd, . . . intimately linked to this relationship is the priest's relationship with the Church. It is not a question of "relations" which are merely juxtaposed, but rather of ones which are interiorly united in a kind of mutual immanence. The priest's relation to the Church is inscribed in the very relation which the priest has to Christ, such that the "sacramental representation" to Christ serves as the basis and inspiration for the relation of the priest to the Church. (par. 16)

Christology is given a priority over ecclesiology in this presentation because the priest must stand before the community and proclaim to it in an authoritative manner the truth of the Gospel. Thus, "the priest is placed not only in the Church, but in the forefront of the Church" (par. 16). However, there is a clear intention not to isolate the priest from the community: "The priesthood ought not to be thought of as existing prior to the Church, because it is totally at the service of the Church. Nor should it be considered as posterior to the ecclesial community, as if the Church could be imagined as already established without this priesthood" (par. 16). There is a strong emphasis on the collegial structure of ordained ministry, on the priest's cooperation with the bishop as a member of a local presbyterate, on his unity with all presbyters because of the sacrament of orders, and on the ordering of ordained priesthood to that of the faithful. Ordained priesthood does not replace that of the faithful but is called to promote it, and a differentiation of roles does not imply two kinds of holiness:

> Indeed the ministerial priesthood does not of itself signify a greater degree of holiness with regard to the common priesthood of the faithful; through it, Christ gives to priests, in the Spirit, a particular gift so that they can help the People of God to exercise faithfully and fully the common priesthood which it has received. (par. 17)

Thus, "the ordained ministry has a radical 'communitarian form' and can only be carried out as a collective work" (par. 17). Moreover, it includes a missionary spirit, a profound concern for and outreach to all the churches and indeed "to the followers of other religions; to people of good will, and in particular to the poor and the defenseless, and to all who yearn, even if they do not know it or cannot express it, for the truth and the salvation of Christ" (par. 17).

The third chapter of the document treats the spirituality of the priesthood. If "all Christians in any state or walk of life are called to the fullness of Christian life and to the perfection of charity," this does not exclude a specific call to holiness for the ordained. One who is called to be a sacramental representation of Christ the Head, one who is thus placed "in the forefront" of the community to call it to holiness is certainly expected to seek the perfection of holiness himself. The specific duties one undertakes as Christ's representative will certainly enter into the orientation of his spiritual life. The document looks at several ways in which this is lived out.

Pastoral charity as the internal principle of the spiritual life of the priest. If ordination configures the priest to Christ in a particular way and grants him special authority for the sake of building up the Body of Christ, then "the spiritual life of the priest is marked, molded, and characterized by the ways of thinking and acting proper to Jesus Christ, Head and Shepherd of the Church, and which are summed up in his pastoral charity" (par. 21). In the ministry of Jesus this pastoral charity can be described first as humble service. Christ has redefined the meaning of Headship precisely in terms of total self-gift: "The spiritual life of the ministers of the New Testament should therefore be marked by this fundamental attitude of service to the People of God, freed from all presumption or desire of 'lording over' those in their charge" (par. 21). The image of shepherd recalls much of the imagery Jesus used in the gospels to describe his compassion, his searching out the lost, his nurturing of his disciples, his willingness to lay down his life. This pastoral charity is further described in terms of Christ's spousal relationship to the church. The priest is also configured to Christ as Bridegroom and sacramentally represents to the church its spouse. This does not separate the priest from the community of the faithful; "he will always remain a member of the community alongside his other brothers and sisters who have been called by the Spirit" (par. 22). Yet, to the extent that he has been placed "in the forefront" of the church,

> the priest's life ought to radiate this spousal character which demands that he be a witness to Christ's spousal love, and thus be capable of loving people with a heart which is new, generous and pure, with genuine self-detachment, with full, constant and faithful dedication, and at the same time with a kind of "divine jealousy," and even with a kind of maternal tenderness, capable of bearing "the pangs of birth" until "Christ be formed" in the faithful. (par. 22)

Pastoral charity, in short, calls the priest to a total, unrestricted gift of himself for the sake of the community. The only way one can hope to give witness to Christ's own love for the church in this kind of service is by one's love for and service to Christ himself: "only in loving and serving Christ the Head and Spouse will charity become a source, criterion, measure and impetus for the priest's love and service to the Church, the Body and Spouse of Christ" (par. 23).[9] Such a self-gift will find its nourishment and its highest expression in the celebration of the Eucharist. If pastoral charity is the fundamental principle of the priest's spiritual life, it is also a dynamic principle of integration and unity, "capable of unifying the many different activities of the priest" (par. 23).

The spiritual life in the exercise of the ministry. In addition to exploring concrete ways in which the exercise of the ministries of Word, sacrament, and pastoral care nourish the spiritual life of the priest, this section speaks of the need for coherence and unity between the priest's life and his ministry. Cultivating a

9. For a discussion of some of the implications of associating celibacy with spousal imagery, cf. David N. Power, "Representing Christ in Community and Sacrament," in Donald Goergen, ed., *Being a Priest Today* (Collegeville, MN: Liturgical Press, 1992), pp. 97–123; and Sarah Butler, "The Priest as Sacrament of Christ the Bridegroom," *Worship* (Nov. 1992), pp. 498–516.

constant awareness or consciousness of one's configuration to Christ will promote responsiveness to the call to holiness. The priest is chosen precisely "as a conscious, free and responsible person," and the more deeply he appropriates the intention "to do in his ministerial activities what the Church intends to do," the more he will himself be transformed:

> This bond tends by its very nature to become as extensive and profound as possible, affecting one's way of thinking, feeling and life itself: in other words, creating a series of moral and spiritual "dispositions" which correspond to the ministerial actions performed by the priest. (par. 25)

Priestly life and the radical call of the Gospel. The evangelical counsels pose a challenge to the life of every Christian, and certainly one who is called to leadership in the church must incorporate these values in a visible way into his spiritual life. Obedience to the will of the one who has sent him is expressed on several levels: an apostolic element related to unity with the pope, the episcopal college, and one's diocesan bishop; a collegial dimension related to unity and co-responsibility with other presbyters, calling one to support and encourage the gifts of others and "not to be bound up in one's own preferences and points of view" (par. 28); and a pastoral character related to the needs and demands of the community (although these demands must be evaluated and tested; it is not assumed that they are always reasonable). Celibate chastity is described in terms of one's configuration to Christ the Head and Spouse of the church:

> The Church, as the Spouse of Jesus Christ, wishes to be loved by the priest in the total and exclusive manner in which Jesus Christ her Head and Spouse loved her. Priestly celibacy, then, is the gift of self *in* and *with* Christ *to* his Church and expresses the priest's service to the Church in and with the Lord. (par. 29)

Poverty is expressed in simplicity of lifestyle that frees the priest to serve where he is needed, in his identification with the poor and the weakest in society, in his responsible administration of the church's goods, and in the challenge of his witness to a world obsessed with money and material security (par. 30).

Membership in and dedication to the particular church. While repeating the conviction that every priest has a concern for the universal church, there is a new stress here on one's belonging to a particular church. Even religious priests exercise their ministry in communion with the local bishop and at the service of a local church. The commitment of incardination is not simply a juridical concept for the sake of structural order but a dimension of one's spiritual life. "The priest finds precisely in his belonging to and dedication to the particular church a wealth of meaning, criteria for discernment and action which shape both his pastoral mission and his spiritual life" (par. 31).[10]

The One Call to Holiness and the States in Life as Different Paths to the Same Goal

The first part of this article speaks about the term *"alter Christus."* If this language has largely disappeared, it is perfectly understandable in light of the way it was used prior to the last council; it certainly tended to posit a different and superior kind of holiness for the ordained. It must be admitted that much of the Sulpician tradition was quite comfortable with this language and its restriction to the clergy. However, this was not so in the first generation of that tradition. Father Olier and the other figures of the first generation of the French school of spirituality certainly had an exalted vision of the priesthood. Nonetheless, they had an even more lofty sense of the dignity that belongs to every Christian because of the sacrament of baptism. They insisted that every Christian is called to holiness and this holiness consists in being more and more configured to Christ. Every Christian should become "another Christ."

---

10. Cf. John R. Donahue, "'The Foolishness of God': New Testament Foundations for a Spirituality of the Priesthood," *Worship* (Nov. 1992), pp. 517–35. In proposing Paul as a model of spirituality, he speaks of the apostle's "engagement with the lived experience of the community" in a way that seems a very practical application of this same principle.

Q: So Jesus Christ dwells in us?

A: Yes, he dwells by faith in our hearts, as Saint Paul says, following the teaching of Our Lord himself.

Q: Didn't you already tell me that we encounter the Holy Spirit there?

A: Yes, he is there with the Father and the Son and there he bestows, as we have said, the very feelings, inclinations, ways and virtues of Jesus Christ.

Q: So then, a Christian is something great?

A: There is nothing greater, nobler or more magnificent. A Christian is a[nother] Jesus Christ living on the earth.[11]

Father Olier had such a strong sense of the indwelling of Christ in the Christian by baptism, that he attributes the good works of Christians to Christ:

> Thus Our Lord is the one who accomplishes every good work in the Church, living in all to honor his Father and using all the faithful like sacraments within which he dwells and acts in different ways for the glory of God. He preaches throughout the world in Saint Paul, who himself says: "It is no longer I who live, but Jesus Christ who lives in me," and again, "Do you desire proof of who it is speaking through me, namely, Jesus Christ?" "*experimentum vultis eius qui in me loquitur Christus.*" It is Our Lord who governs the Church in Saint Peter. It is he who takes care of his mother in Saint John, after his death. Once again, even before his birth, it is he who prepared himself a precursor and gave him some of his spirit and his zeal, the same gifts which he had already poured out on Elijah who is to be the forerunner of his final coming.[12]

11. J.-J. Olier, *Christian Catechism for the Interior Life*, Lesson III. The translation is mine.

12. J.-J. Olier, "Living Sacraments of Jesus Christ," in *Living for God in Christ Jesus*, an anthology of the writings of Father Olier, published privately for the United States Province of the Society of Saint Sulpice, p. 23.

If every Christian is "another Christ," and if the priest represents Christ, renders Christ present in the world, as the head and shepherd of his church, how do other Christians render him present? I believe that recent documents coming from the synods on the laity and on religious life work well in conjunction with Father Olier's fundamental insights on Christian anthropology to clarify the different (not superior and inferior) ways of being Christ in the world. All three states in life can make Christians "living sacraments." All three can serve to lead us to the one holiness to which all are called. This truth is reaffirmed in *Christifideles Laici*, the document published in 1994 by Pope John Paul II as the fruit of the Synod on the Laity:

> In Church Communion the states of life, by being ordered one to the other, are thus bound together among themselves. They all share in a deeply basic meaning: that of being the manner of living out the commonly shared Christian dignity and the universal call to holiness in the perfection of love. They are different yet complementary in the sense that each of them has a basic and unmistakable character which sets each apart, while at the same time each of them is seen in relation to the other and placed at each other's service.
>
> Thus the lay state of life has its distinctive feature in its secular character. It fulfills an ecclesial service in bearing witness and, in its own way recalling for priests, women and men religious, the significance of the earthly and temporal realities in the salvific plan of God. In turn, the ministerial priesthood represents in different times and places, the permanent guarantee of the sacramental presence of Christ the Redeemer. The religious state bears witness to the eschatological character of the Church, that is, the straining towards the Kingdom of God that is prefigured and in some way anticipated and experienced even now through the vows of chastity, poverty and obedience.[13]

The lay faithful are living sacraments of Christ who transforms the world, who confronts the values of the world (in the Fourth

---

13. *Christifideles Laici*, par. 55.

Gospel's sense of the term) and promotes the values of the kingdom, who protects the dignity of every person, who works for justice and peace. By their way of living and working in the world, Christian lay faithful bear witness by their words and actions to the values of God's kingdom. They can also exercise a positive influence by their participation in public life.

The above citation also speaks of the state of life of consecrated religious. They are called to be living sacraments of Christ who has definitively introduced the Kingdom of God into the world through his own life and ministry. He continues to live the values of that Kingdom through those who have committed themselves publicly to live the values of the Kingdom here and now. The life of the evangelical counsels lived in a radical commitment together with the values of the beatitudes reflects already the renewed humanity that will be fulfilled at the end of time.

In speaking of such a sacramental vision of the various states of life, it is important to recognize that the distinctions between three ways of representing Christ, of being living sacraments of Christ, are not mutually exclusive. Obviously, priests are not the only ones who exercise roles of leadership in the church. It is evident that many women religious, brothers, and laypeople serve in important capacities of leadership. In fact, since the priesthood of the ordained is "ordered to" the priesthood of the faithful, it is natural that priests and bishops foster and encourage people to take on such responsibilities. However, such is not their primary focus or obligation. Likewise, all Christians, not just consecrated religious, are to integrate into their lives the values of the Kingdom of God, the evangelical counsels, and the beatitudes. However, we need in the church people who live those values in a radical way precisely to challenge the rest of us to find ways to incorporate them in our lives. Finally, religious and priests share a concern for the transformation of the world. But the "secular" sphere is more properly a primary concern or duty for the lay faithful.

Some Concluding Reflections and Questions

After this brief examination of the broad lines of the theology of ordained ministry in *Pastores Dabo Vobis*, it is possible to draw some conclusions and to raise some questions. We will limit ourselves here to (1) a brief comparison of the Tridentine and current Vatican approaches to priestly identity; (2) some of the chief features of priestly spirituality; (3) some questions about permanence of priesthood in light of recent events; and (4) a question about configuration to Christ the head and religious priesthood.

Trent and Vatican II on Priestly Identity

It may be observed that there is strong continuity between the emerging consensus on priestly identity as a configuration to Christ the Head of the church and the Tridentine definition. It would be hard to imagine the council fathers at Trent objecting to this language. At the same time, recent Vatican statements clearly have in view the (largely unintended)[14] limitations of the previous definition of priestly identity and have attempted to avoid falling into the same problems. The narrow sacramental focus of the previous definition is replaced with a clear vision that ordained apostolic ministry necessarily includes the three elements of proclamation, sacramental celebration, and pastoral care or leadership. There are clear statements that all share by virtue of baptism and confirmation in the priesthood of Christ and that all seek the same holiness and perfection of charity; there is a fundamental equality and dignity of all believers. The priesthood of the ordained is not intended to replace that of the faithful but to promote it. If the presbyter is placed in the forefront of the church, other statements caution against elitism or isolation of

14. This is not the place for discussion of the hermeneutics of conciliar statements, but I would argue that the narrow sacramental focus for priesthood in Trent's document on sacraments is balanced by the reform decree's call for good preaching and pastoral care, that the failure to assert the importance of the priesthood of the faithful was not intended as a denial of it but that Trent's primary concern was to reaffirm what was denied by the reformers, etc. Whether the council fathers believed in a different and superior kind of holiness for the ordained would probably be a more complicated question. Certainly, they had no intention of compromising the one priesthood of Christ in asserting the divine institution of an ordained priesthood nor did they intend to deny the laity's direct access to God in prayer.

the priest from the life of the community. It may also be argued that such caution is more than pious exhortation to humility because of two factors: the defining of the Headship of Christ in terms of service and the rooting of ministerial identity in the Trinity.

A series of articles begun in *Theological Studies* in 1994 takes a critical look at this notion of configuration to Christ the Head of the church from the perspective of the scholastics' use of the phrase *in persona Christi capitis ecclesiae*. Dennis Ferrara argues that the use of the concept in recent documents of the magisterium is really quite different from its original use in Thomas Aquinas and other authors of the Middle Ages. Whereas it has taken on a representational sense in recent statements (the priest is a sacramental representative of Christ in his task of leadership), it was originally used, according to Ferrara, in a self-effacing sense. What mattered for Thomas was not the priest's ability to represent Christ but rather the fact that the priest is merely an instrument used by Christ.[15] Consequently, it was the priest's difference from Christ that was most important. The series of articles by Ferrara is carefully presented and makes some interesting points. A critical look at Ferrara's position by Sara Butler is also very impressive. What seems important to this reader is that this is a viable theological position. Moreover, it is now, because of its inclusion in documents of the magisterium, the official position. Is it definitive? It is not claimed to be so. It is a

15. Cf. Dennis Michael Ferrara, "Representation or Self-Effacement: The Axiom *In Persona Christi* in Thomas Aquinas and the Magisterium," *Theological Studies*, vol. 55 (1994), pp. 195–224; Dennis M. Ferrara, "Note: The Ordination of Women: Tradition and Meaning," *Theological Studies*, vol. 55, pp. 706–719; Sara Butler, "*Quaestio Disputata:* '*In Persona Christi*': A Response to Dennis M. Ferrara," *Theological Studies*, vol. 56 (1995), pp. 61–80; Dennis M. Ferrara, " '*In Persona Christi*': A Reply to Sara Butler," *Theological Studies*, vol. 56, pp. 81–91. Another series of articles dealing with the same question appeared in *Worship*. Cf. Susan K. Wood, "Priestly Identity: Sacrament of the Ecclesial Community," *Worship*, vol. 69 (1995), pp. 109–26; Sara Butler, "Priestly Identity: 'Sacrament' of Christ the Head," *Worship*, vol. 70 (1996), pp. 290–306; Lawrence J. Welch, "Priestly Identity Reconsidered: A Reply to Susan Wood," *Worship*, vol. 70 (1996), pp. 307–18.

theological explanation, not a dogmatic definition. The last theological position lasted for almost eight hundred years (if we take it back to Aquinas), and it flourished despite the limitations that accompanied it. If the contemporary position, as presented by Pope John Paul II, is not the final word, it is the only reasonable candidate that has been presented yet as a contemporary expression of the distinctiveness of ordained priesthood in relation to the royal priesthood of the baptized. At least this time the pope is quite aware of its limitations and has tried to build into the notion of configuration to Christ the Head a corrective to some of its potential abuses.

Every priest needs, perhaps, to recognize as well that the presbyterate as a whole will project this vision of ordained ministry much better than any individual will.

Some of the Features of Priestly Spirituality

The new Catechism does not treat the question of a "priestly" spirituality, but *Pastores Dabo Vobis* does so at length. It should be noted that much of what is described in the third chapter of the apostolic exhortation would apply to the whole community of believers: all are called to put on Christ and to have the attitude that was in Christ, all are called to service, all should reflect the evangelical counsels in their lives, etc. If the priesthood of the ordained is ordered to that of the faithful, then part of its task will be the cultivation of the same qualities in the larger community. Nonetheless, one can easily acknowledge that those called to leadership in the community will find a particular call and challenge in the ordinary exercise of their ministerial duties, and we can speak of a "specific vocation to holiness" for the ordained. Its features include the following, though it must be acknowledged that each of these principles applies in some way to the spiritual life of every disciple.

It must be solidly christological. Pastores Dabo Vobis tells us "the spiritual life of the priest is marked, molded, and characterized by the ways of thinking and acting proper to Jesus Christ, Head and Shepherd of the Church" (par. 21). Not only the study of Christology (especially the mission and ministry of Jesus) but a prayer life formed around the Word of God proclaimed in the Scriptures will be central.[16]

It must be ecclesial in at least the following senses. It is collegial in the bonds that link the priest to other ordained ministers. It is immersed in the lives of those the ordained priest is called to serve. It is a spirituality of public witness: the one who is to sacramentalize the presence of Christ the Head, Shepherd, and the Spouse of the church cannot think of his spiritual life as something entirely private.

It will find both expression and nourishment in a life of humble service. So, of course, will every Christian's spiritual life, since all share in the mission and priestliness of Christ; but the ordained priest's spirituality will reflect certain features precisely because of his ministerial duties and his call to represent Christ the Head. Since Christ's own headship is defined in terms of humble service, there will be no room for self-importance in those who are to render Christ visible precisely in his headship.

Questions about Permanence in the Sacrament of Orders in Light of Recent Events

A question about spirituality arises from the departure from the active ministry of a significant number of priests in the first few years after ordination. This concern has been with us for a number of years. Sociologist Dean Hoge deals with the causes of the problem in a study titled *The First Five Years of Priesthood.*[17] He observes that those who leave generally have two things in common: isolation and the sense that they are not appreciated. It seems that priests can live with one or with the other of these two burdens, but the combination is particularly dangerous. This is a point that should be underlined with bishops, seminary formators, and diocesan personnel boards. George Aschenbrenner, in a book on

---

16. Cf. Kenan Osborne, *op. cit.*, p. 334.

17. Dean Hoge, *The First Five Years of Priesthood* (Collegeville, MN: Liturgical Press, 2002).

priestly spirituality, suggests a practical method for helping seminarians advance toward a lifelong commitment.[18]

A theological question concerning permanence arises from the recent scandals and the frequent reduction to the lay state of priests guilty of cases of sexual abuse of minors. What are the theological implications of these reductions? In light of a theology of priesthood that stresses the sacramental representation of Christ the Head of the church, are there some acts that so hinder this representation for the people of God that the priest simply cannot be allowed to exercise the ministry again?[19] Is permanence now limited to the fact that if one day it is discovered that a priest who was reduced to the lay state was falsely accused, he would be readmitted to priesthood without a new ceremony of ordination?[20]

A Question about Configuration to Christ the Head and a Question about Religious Priests

Configuration to Christ the Head. Does this statement of the identity of the priest privilege parochial ministry and relegate other priests to a marginal identity? What of the priest whose ministry is exercised primarily in the classroom or the hospital chaplain who serves the most transient of communities?[21] Perhaps a solution can be found in recognizing that the primary analogue of ordained priesthood is the office of bishop; all presbyters, regardless of their ministry, share in priesthood on a second level as cooperators with the bishops.

18. George Aschenbrenner, *Quickening the Fire Within* (Chicago: Loyola Press, 2003).

19. Cf. George Weigel, *The Courage to be Catholic* (New York: Basic Books, 2002).

20. For a very interesting interpretation of the background to these scandals in the United States, cf. Howard P. Bleichner, *View from the Altar* (New York: Crossroad, 2004).

21. Related to this is another question. Does not this representation of Christ the Head apply more to the lay leaders of local communities than to such priests whose duties do not include pastoral leadership?

Religious priests. Several articles have been written in recent years about priests in religious communities, speaking of historical differences in their exercise of the ministry. It has been pointed out, for example, that religious priests have been more oriented toward missionary outreach, that their poverty has enabled them to identify with and serve as advocates for social justice, that preaching and evangelization pushed them more toward a prophetic than a cultic ministry.[22] The documents acknowledge the unique contributions to ministry and the life of the church that have resulted from the charisms of religious communities.[23] However, there is very little mention of religious priests, and both documents stress their cooperation with the diocesan bishop and presbyterate. Perhaps this will be an area in which the understanding of the collegial nature of presbyteral ministry can be helpful. For one thing, we might say that religious priests kept alive within the priesthood a strong missionary focus and a strong commitment to preaching at moments when most diocesan priests saw their ministry as almost exclusively local and cultic. However, at a time when priesthood as such is seen as comprehensive and includes a commitment to all these issues, no priest can dismiss or ignore a missionary focus, preaching, or social justice. Still, one must acknowledge that in a collegial body of presbyters, a Maryknoll missioner is going to manifest the commitment to mission much more clearly than most local pastors.

---

22. Cf., e.g., John O'Malley, "Priesthood, Ministry, and Religious Life: Some Historical and Historiographical Considerations," *Theological Studies*, vol. 49 (1988), 223–57; Paul J. Philibert, "Priesthood within the Context of Religious Life," in Donald Goergen, ed., *Being a Priest Today* (Collegeville, MN: Liturgical Press, 1992), pp. 73–96; and Thomas P. Rausch, "Priesthood in Apostolic Religious Communities," in *Priesthood Today: An Appraisal* (New York: Paulist Press, 1992), pp. 82–104.

23. Cf., e.g., *Pastores Dabo Vobis*, par. 31, and the *Catechism*, par. 927.

Chapter 3

"Faithful Stewards of God's Mysteries": Theological Insights on Priesthood from the Ordination Ritual

Rev. Michael G. Witczak, SLD

Introduction

The Year for Priests called by Pope Benedict XVI leads me to reflect on my own journey to the priesthood. When I was in grade school, one part of the attraction was watching the priest celebrate Mass at St. Robert Church in Shorewood, Wisconsin. The whole environment of the liturgy: the music (mixed in quality as it was!), the stained glass, the vestments, the smells, the sounds (rustling and murmuring of children, clickers of nuns, bells, kneelers) drew me to want to be immersed in the experience. And I knew that everyone liked Father. (It was only a week into my first assignment as a priest that I learned that was not true!)

As I began seminary studies and eventually specialized in liturgical studies, my awareness of the contexts and texts of the liturgy[1] has led me to reflect on how the liturgy is a place to look for a theology of priesthood, both in the celebrations led by priests and in the liturgy of ordaining priests.

---

1. See Kevin W. Irwin, *Context and Text: Method in Liturgical Theology* (Collegeville, MN: Liturgical Press, A Pueblo Book, 1994); Peter E. Fink, "Three Languages of Christian Sacrament," in *Worship: Praying the Sacraments* (Washington, DC: Pastoral Press, 1991), 29–44.

Scope and Limits of This Talk

This time together, necessarily limited, will focus on two areas: an overview of the whole celebration of the ordination of priests and the prayer of ordination from the rite of ordination of priests.

The Ordination Ritual

Some Notes from History

Roman simplicity: imposition of hands and prayer of consecration (the Ordines Romani). An early liturgical record of ordination comes from the document known as the Apostolic Tradition.[2] There the heart of the celebration is the imposition of hands on the one to be ordained a presbyter while a prayer of consecration is said. At the time of the Second Vatican Council and the reform of the liturgy, most scholars accepted the attribution of the Apostolic Tradition to Hippolytus of Rome. More recently the attribution has been questioned by Marcel Metzger, Paul Bradshaw, and others.[3] The presence of a central ritual of imposition of hands with prayer remains the key moment in the fourth-century Latin translation, regardless of provenance.

Additions to the Roman core. The Ordines Romani, gathered by Michel Andrieu in the middle part of the twentieth century, reveal the development of the ordination ritual in the early Middle Ages. The Roman core ritual remains imposition of hands with prayer. Frankish additions include the *traditio instrumentorum*

---

2. See the edition by Bernard Botte, *La Tradition apostolique de Saint Hippolyte: Essai de reconstitution*, 5th ed. by Albert Gerhards with Sabine Felbecker, *Liturgiewissenschaftliche Quellen und Forschungen* 39 (Münster Westfalen: Aschendorff, 1961, 1989).

3. See bibliography in Paul F. Bradshaw, Maxwell E. Johnson, and L. Edward Phillips, *The Apostolic Tradition: A Commentary*, edited by Harold W. Attridge (Minneapolis: Fortress Press, 2002). However, see also the treatments of Wilhelm Geerlings in *Didache - Zwölf-apostel-Lehre/Traditio Apostolica - Apostolische Überlieferung, Fontes Christiani* 1 (Freiburg: Herder, 1991); and Hippolytus, *On the Apostolic Tradition*, ed. by Alistair Stewart-Sykes, Popular Patristics Series 22 (Crestwood, NY: St. Vladimir's Seminary Press, 2001).

(the handing over of bread and wine from the bishop to the one being ordained) and an anointing of hands.[4]

Medieval theological reflection on matter and form. The additions seemed to speak more clearly of the meaning of the ritual of ordination than the handlaying and prayer. By the time we reach St. Thomas and the subsequent use of his work as the basis for the Decree for the Armenians, the *traditio instrumentorum* has become identified as the essential matter and form of ordination of priests for a number of theologians. The 1439 Decree says: "Its matter is that by the handing over (*traditio*) of which the Order is conferred: thus the presbyterate is conferred by handing over (*porrectio*) the chalice with wine and the paten with bread."[5]

Redefinition of matter and form by Pope Pius XII (1947). The question of the matter and form of the sacrament of orders and the related question whether bishops are ordained or simply have a higher form of jurisdiction was finally settled by Pope Pius XII in his Apostolic Constitution *Sacramentum Ordinis* of 1947. The pope decreed that the matter and form of all three sacraments is the imposition of hands and the prayer accompanying it. In addition, the *traditio* is not required for the valid celebration of the sacraments.

The reforms of Vatican II. The bishops gathered at the Second Vatican Council (1962–1965) spoke briefly about the need to reform the liturgy of ordination in the Constitution on the Sacred

---

4. Andrieu considers Ordo 34 to be Roman, and orders 35 and 36 to be Roman with Frankish additions. See Michel Andrieu, *Les Ordines Romani du haut moyen age*, 5 vols., *Spicilegium Sacrum Lovaniense, Études et Documents* 11, 23, 24, 28, and 29 (Louvain: Spicilegium Sacrum Lovaniense, 1930–1961), III:533–619, and IV: 1–110.

5. Eugene IV, Bull *Exsultate Deo* of 22 November 1439. See J. Neuner and J. Dupuis, *The Christian Faith in the Doctrinal Documents of the Catholic Church*, edited by Jacques Dupuis, 6th ed. (New York: Alba House, 1996), 671 = H. Denzinger and A. Schönmetzer, *Enchiridion Symbolorum, Definitionum et Declarationum de rebus fidei et morum*, 36th ed. (Freiburg: Herder, 1976), n. 1326, p. 336. This document is based on the teaching of St. Thomas Aquinas as found in his *De articulis fidei et Ecclesiae sacramentis*; see the notes in Denzinger-Schönmetzer above.

Liturgy.[6] They treated the General Principles for the Reform of the Liturgy, including the nature and importance of the liturgy, the promotion of liturgical instruction and active participation, and various general norms for the reform of the liturgy. They concluded the opening chapter by speaking of the promotion of liturgical life and action. Two chapters follow on the sacraments: one on the Mass, the other on the rest of the sacraments and the sacramentals.

The treatment of the sacrament of orders is brief: "Both the ceremonies and texts of the ordination rites are to be revised" (n. 76). This must be understood within the context of the whole first chapter of the Constitution and the introductory paragraphs of chapter 3, "The Other Sacraments and the Sacramentals." In particular, the bishops point out that there is a threefold purpose of sacraments. First, they make people holy. Second, they build up the body of Christ. Third, they give worship to God. As signs they also teach. They presuppose faith but also nourish and strengthen it. They confer grace but also dispose the reception of grace in their celebration (n. 59). The grace flows from the paschal mystery of Christ's passion, death, and resurrection (n. 61). Elements have entered the celebration over time that have made the nature and purpose of the sacraments less clear to today's believer, and so changes have become necessary (n. 62).

Typical editions: 1968 and 1990. The very first ritual to be issued was the Rite for Ordaining Deacons, Priests, and Bishops. Pope Paul VI issued an Apostolic Constitution, *Pontificalis Romani recognitio,* 18 June 1968, and the ritual was issued by the Congregation of Rites on 15 August 1968. It is important to remember that this ritual predates the new calendar, the new missal and lectionary, and other decisions affecting the sacrament of orders, such as the subdiaconate and minor orders. As elements of the reform continued to unfold, the ritual came under some criticism: the lack of a substantial introduction such as can be found in the

6. See text in *Documents of the Liturgy 1963–1979: Conciliar, Papal, and Curial Texts* (Collegeville, MN: Liturgical Press, 1982), 4–27. Vatican Council II, Constitution on the Liturgy (*Sacrosantum Concilium*), 4 December 1963: AAS 56 (1964): 97–138.

other liturgical books, the order of the book (starting with deacons), the decision to leave the ancient prayers for the ordination of presbyters and deacons, and other elements.[7] A particular criticism of the prayer for the ordination of priests was that it retained civic language from ancient Rome little understood today and that the theology of the church and of the priesthood from the documents of the Second Vatican Council was not articulated. Work on a second edition began already in 1973 but was delayed in 1975. It was taken up again in the 1980s and a second typical edition issued in 1989 (published in 1990).

This brief historical sketch does not take the place of a complete history of the celebration of the sacrament of holy orders.[8] However, it does give us a sense of the ebb and flow of the rites of ordination of a priest, though it has not touched on the complications that entered the rite of ordination of presbyters, including investiture in presbyteral vestments, concelebration, recitation of the Credo, the second imposition of hands with the phrase *Accipe spiritum sanctum*, and the promise of obedience.

The Ordination Ritual: Its Structure and Some Comments

We now move to a consideration of the current rite of ordination of a priest. We will look at two elements. The first will be a look at the overall structure of the rite.

The second part will be a closer reading of the prayer of ordination of a priest.

First we will look at the overall structure of the rite.

7. See the account in Annibale Bugnini, *The Reform of the Liturgy 1948–1975*, tr. Matthew J. O'Connell (Collegeville, MN: Liturgical Press, 1990), 707–23.

8. See, for instance, Kenan B. Osborne, *Priesthood: A History of the Ordained Ministry in the Roman Catholic Church* (New York: Paulist Press, 1988); James Puglisi, *The Process of Admission to Ordained Ministry: A Comparative Study*, 3 volumes (Collegeville, MN: Liturgical Press, A Pueblo Book, 1996, 1998, 2001); Bruno Kleinheyer, "Ordinationen und Beauftragungen," in *Sakramentliche Feiern II*, Volume 8 of *Gottesdienst der Kirche: Handbuch der Liturgiewissenschaft*, ed. by Hans Bernhard Meyer et al., pp. 7–65 (Regensburg: Pustet, 1983). A helpful historical overview is contained in Salvador Pie, "La Plegaria de ordenación de los presbíteros: Nueva edición del Ritual," *Phase* 186 (1991) 471–90, especially 472–75.

Structure

1. Introductory Rites and Liturgy of the Word (there are special orations)

2. Ordination

    a. Election of the Candidates

        (1) Call by deacon

        (2) Presentation by a designated priest

        (3) Election by the bishop

        (4) Assent of the people

    b. Homily

    c. Promise of the Elect

    Work with the bishop

    The ministry of the word

    The Ministry of the Sacraments, especially the Eucharist and Reconciliation

    Prayer

    Consecration to Christ

    Obedience (placing hands within those of the bishop)

  Litany of Supplication (Litany of the Saints)

  Laying On of Hands and Prayer of Ordination

  Anointing of Hands and Handing Over of the Bread and Wine: this begins with vesting the newly ordained in the vestments of a priest for Mass and ends with the sharing of the sign of peace with the bishop and other priests present

Liturgy of the Eucharist: there is a special preface and intercessions for the Eucharistic Prayer

Concluding Rites: there is a special final blessing

Some comments.[9] In general, the structure of the rite of ordination of priests, as we will also see in the structure of the prayer of ordination, takes us from the past into the present of the cele-

9. I acknowledge conversations with and the notes of Kenneth Smits, former professor of liturgy at St. Francis Seminary in Milwaukee.

bration and projects us into the future, both the immediate future in the celebration of the Eucharist and then entering into the life of presbyteral service, as well as the eschatological future of life lived forever in God.

Overview

There are four major sections in the rite of ordination of priests:

2a-b: Election, recalling the biblical pattern of call and response and actualizing it today

2c-d: Promise and Litany, ritualizing and summing up the process of formation and actualizing its implications

2e: the heart of the ritual, the Laying On of Hands and Prayer of Ordination, the Holy Spirit invoked and conferred for ministry (we will spend more time with this in the next section)

2f: ritualizes the unfolding complexity of the ministry that has been accepted, projecting it into the Eucharist about to be celebrated

Commentary

Some specific comments follow. The Election of the Candidates (2a above) can be seen as ritualizing the biblical pattern of call and response (e.g., Moses in Exodus 3:1-6, and Samuel in 1 Samuel 3:2-10). Another strand found here is that of election: I will be your God and you will be my people. The election moves from the people of Israel (see, for example, the covenant ceremony described in Exod 24), to Jesus ("You are my beloved Son," Mark 1:11 par.; cf. Mark 9:7 par., the transfiguration), to the Church (You are the body of Christ and individually members of it, 1 Cor 12:27). The spirit of call and election remains a part of the dynamic of the Christian life, seen generally in baptism and specifically in marriage and holy orders (and outside of the sacraments in the rites of consecrating virgins and of religious profession).

This call is closely connected to the Liturgy of the Word celebrated in the church and celebrated at the liturgy of ordination. The word proclaimed and explained to the people of God is always a word that demands a response. That response takes concrete form in this celebration in the call and response of the candidates for ordination, as well as in the Eucharist and beyond it in Christian living.

The affirmation of the election by the assembled faithful calls to mind that the whole community has a stake in the life of the church. While there could be overtones of recent "reality shows" like *American Idol*, in fact this acclamation by the people is rooted in the history of the church and the conviction that the ones chosen to lead have an intimate reciprocal bond with the whole body of Christ.

Note that all the orders of the church are involved: a deacon calls the candidates; a priest presents them to the bishop; the bishop elects them; the gathered faithful acclaim the election. This is an act of the whole local church.

The homily has as its general and overall goal the explaining of the word that has been proclaimed and of revealing God's presence in all that is occurring in the celebration of the sacrament.[10] The homily serves as the transition from the Liturgy of the Word to the Liturgy of the Sacrament and forms part of the dynamic of the transition: what God has done as told in the Scriptures continues to take place in our midst today. The call received by those in the past is heard today by others, and the response that was made in the past is taken up anew by new hearers. The homily reveals how this is happening. The placement of the homily after the call and election ensures that the elect are the particular hearers of the word.

The next section of the celebration (2c in the outline above) is the promise of the elect. It ritualizes and sums up the years of formation of the candidate. That formation included human, spiritual, intellectual, and pastoral components (see John Paul II, apostolic exhortation, *Pastores Dabo Vobis*, 25 March 1992,

---

10. See the General Instruction of the Roman Missal [2002], n. 65; Introduction to the Lectionary, n. 24.

nn. 43–59;[11] *Program of Priestly Formation*, 5th ed., nn. 68–257).[12] The questions and the affirmative responses of the candidates for ordination recapitulate all that has taken place in their formation.

The heart of the ritual is the laying on of hands and the prayer of ordination. The gesture, found in Scripture, is the traditional sign of the sharing of roles of responsibility for the good of the church. It speaks of the descent of the Holy Spirit, and joined to the prayer names the event that is taking place through God's grace. The next section will explore the text of the prayer in some detail.

The explanatory rites attempt to symbolize all the laying on of hands and prayer have done. The taking on of priestly vestments, anointing of the hands of the newly ordained, handing over to the paten with bread and the chalice with wine, and the sign of peace focus mainly on the role of the priest in celebrating the Eucharist on behalf the church. The sign of peace holds up the bond with bishop and the fraternity of the priesthood. However, the roles of governance and preaching do not find much expression in the explanatory rites.

Much more could be said about the ritual dynamics and the specific texts of the ordination ritual. The ritual structure of Liturgy of the Word, Liturgy of Ordination, and Liturgy of the Eucharist implies a certain theology in and of itself. The Liturgy of the Word proclaims God's word into the midst of the assembly of believers and the homily actualizes it in the context of holy orders and the Eucharist. The Liturgy of Ordination celebrates the gift of leadership, calls candidates forward, rehearses their preparation, and in the great prayer of ordination brings them from past to present and injects them into the life of the church. The Liturgy of the Eucharist then provides the context for the gifts of the community, those who have just been called from its midst and ordained, and likewise the bread and wine. The new

11. In *Norms for Priestly Formation*, Volume II (Washington, DC: United States Catholic Conference, 1994), 306–22.

12. In *Program of Priestly Formation*, Fifth Edition (Washington, DC: United States Conference of Catholic Bishops, 2006), 28–85.

priests together with the bishop and their confreres in the presbyterate take the gifts, bless them in the Eucharistic Prayer, break
them during the Lamb of God, and distribute them in Holy Communion. All are then sent forth "to love and serve the Lord." The
Food for the Journey (*viaticum*) is the source of the life of the new
priests and the community of believers from which they have
been called and to which they are sent to serve.

Some interesting similarities and differences can be seen when
comparing the structure of ordination to the structure of baptism.
Both have a calling by name and response, both involve promises
and the use of the litany, both include explanatory rites (new
clothes, an anointing, the handing over of a symbol of new life
[candle, and bread and wine]). Both include a prayer of blessing,
but here the parallel breaks down. In baptism the great blessing
is over the water that will be used to baptize. In ordination, it is the
blessing and the handlaying that form the central act of the rite.

Both are inaugurations into a new life: baptism into the new
life in Christ as a member of his body washed clear of sin; ordination into the new life of service to that body as a collaborator with
the bishop. The theology of character, the permanent, essential
change that the sacrament brings about, is at play here.

The Ordination Ritual: The Prayer of Consecration of a Priest (Comparison with 1968 Prayer)

Historical Notes

The prayer contained in the current rite of ordination of priests
is an emendation of the prayer that occurs in its earliest form in
the *Sacramentarium Veronense*, a compilation of individual book-
lets for the celebration of Mass (*missarum libelli*) made in the sixth
century. and now contained in a manuscript in the Verona
Capitular Library. The text was then taken up into the classic
Roman sacramentaries and pontificals. In its transmission it took
on a preferred form of the medieval Roman Rite, adopting the
form of a preface for the prayer, including the dialogue and using
the sung tone familiar to the preface form.[13]

---

13. In more or less chronological order, see: Leo Cunibert Mohlberg, Leo
Eizenhöfer, and Petrus Siffrin, eds., *Sacramentarium Veronense (Cod. Bibl. Capit.*

The first typical edition in 1968 left the text from the Veronense largely intact, since it was considered to be text that was theologically substantial. There were several emendations, following the criteria given in the Constitution on the Liturgy mentioned above. An introductory prayer was omitted, the language of the preface was omitted, and the conclusion of the prayer was changed to include a reference to the ministry of the word, so important in the documents of Vatican II (see, e.g., PO 4: "Priests, therefore, as the co-workers of the bishops, have for their first responsibility the proclaiming of God's Gospel to all").[14]

This first liturgical book of the reform received some criticism.[15] Among the criticisms were that the prayer for the ordination of priests was deficient in its theology, especially in light of the teachings of the Second Vatican Council. The second typical edition, begun in the early 1970s and finally issued in 1990, tries to address these concerns.

Veron. LXXXV [80]), Rerum Ecclesiasticarum Documenta [=RED], Series Maior, Fontes I, 3rd ed. (Rome: Herder, 1954, 1994), n. 954, p. 121; Leo Cunibert Mohlberg, Leo Eizenhöfer, and Petrus Siffrin, eds., *Liber Sacramentorum romanae aeclesiae ordinis anni circuli (Cod. Vat. Reg. Lat. 316/Paris, Bibl Nat. 7193, 41/56) (Sacramentarium Gelasianum),* RED Fontes IV, 3rd ed. (Rome: Herder, 1960, 1981), n. 145–46, pp. 25–26; Jean Deshusses, *Le Sacramentaire Grégorien: Ses principales formes d'après les plus anciens manuscrits,* Vol. I, 3rd ed., Spicilegium Friburgense 16 (Fribourg, Switzerland: Éditions Universitaires, 1971, 1992), n. 29, pp. 95–96; Cyrille Vogel and Reinhard Elze, *Le Pontifical Romano-Germanique du dixième siècle: Le texte I (nn. I-XCVIII),* Studi e Testi 226 (Vatican City: Biblioteca Apostolica Vaticana, 1963), n. 29, pp. 33–34; Michel Andrieu, *Le Pontifical Romain au moyen-age, Tome III: Le Pontifical de Guillaume Durand,* Studi e Testi 88 (Vatican City: Biblioteca Apostolica Vaticana, 1940), Book I, XIII:9, p. 368. The text enters the Roman Pontifical, issued in 1595/96. See Manlio Sodi and Achille Maria Triacca, eds., *Pontificale Romanum: Editio Princeps (1595–1596),* Monumenta Liturgica Concilii Tridentini 1 (Vatican City: Libreria Editrice Vaticana, 1997), nn. 110–12, pp. 65–71; and the final edition of the Roman Pontifical prior to the Second Vatican Council, Manlio Sodi and Alessandro Toniolo, eds., *Pontificale Romanum: Editio Typica 1961–1962,* Monumenta Liturgica Piana 3 (Vatican City: Libreria Editrice Vaticana, 2008), nn. 154–159, pp. 49–52.

14. DOL, n. 259, p. 72.

15. See the summary in Jan Michael Joncas, "The Public Language Ministry Revisited: *De Ordinatione Episcopi, Presbyterorum et Diaconorum 1990, Worship* 68 (1994): 386–403; criticisms listed on 386–92.

In our treatment, we will first discuss the structure of the prayer and then offer a commentary, using a comparison with the 1968 text as a point of reference.

Structure of the Prayer

The prayer has been analyzed in several ways by various authors since its appearance, each offering a slightly different approach to the structure. We will build on their work and offer yet another way of understanding how the prayer is structured.

A first way to approach structure is rooted in the analysis offered of the Eucharistic Prayer tradition by Italian Jesuit Cesare Giraudo.[16] He sees these great prayers as having two main parts: the anamnetic part and the epicletic. The anamnetic is a recalling of the great deeds that God has done on behalf of his people. The epicletic moves from remembering to petition, asking that God act on our behalf today, in a way consistent with what has been remembered. The prayer of ordination follows that same structure. The anamnetic section is the first part up to ll. 37-38: "carry out the work of salvation throughout the whole world." The epicletic section begins immediately, l. 39: "And now we beseech you." The move from remembering to asking is marked by the transitional phrase "And now."

Another overarching analysis would emphasize the trinitarian dimension of the prayer and see it in three major parts: Anamnesis of the work of the Father, Epiclesis of the Holy Spirit, Intercession through Jesus Christ, concluding with a trinitarian doxology.[17] Here is an overview of the structure:

---

16. Cesare Giraudo, *La struttura letteraria della preghiera eucaristica: Saggio sulla genesi letteraria di una forma: toda veterotestamentaria, beraka guidaica, anafora cristiana*, Analecta Biblica 92 (Rome: Biblical Institute Press, 1981).

17. See the work of Giuseppe Ferraro in *Le preghiere di ordinazione al diaconato, al presbiterato, all'episcopato* (Naples: Edizioni Dehoniane, 1977); and his updated work in "La nuova preghiera di ordinazione presbiterale," *Civiltà Cattolica* 141/3 (1990): 26–39. See the slightly different analysis of Salvador Pie, "La plegaria de ordenación de los presbíteros: Nueva edición del Ritual," *Phase* 186 (1991): 479.

Anamnesis of the Father's work

A. ll. 1-6: Prologue: invocation and the naming of God's salvific attributes and acts

B. ll. 7-10: Anamnesis I (OT): the various grades of minstry in support of Moses and Aaron

C. ll. 12-17: Anamnesis II (OT): Moses and the 70: governing

D. ll. 19-21: Anamnesis III (OT): Aaron and his sons: worship

E. ll. 23-38: Anamnesis IV (NT): Jesus and the Apostles: ministry of sharing Christ's mission

Epiclesis of the Holy Spirit

F. ll. 39-41: Transition from anamnesis to today (which Ferraro calls the "actualization")

G. ll. 43-51: Epiclesis of the Holy Spirit (see Pius XII, Apostolic Constitution)

Intercession through Jesus Christ the Son

H. ll. 53-57: Petition I: that he be a co-worker and preacher

I. ll. 60-65: Petition II: that he be steward of the mysteries (sacramental ministry)

J. ll. 66-69: Petition III: that he pray for the whole world

Doxology of the Trinity

K. ll. 71-73: Eschatological transition

L. ll. 74-77: Final doxological praise and response of the people

Commentary

In the commentary that follows, we will pause at the places that have seen changes in this new edition.[18] In the accompanying

---

18. A number of helpful commentaries on the prayer of ordination of priests have appeared over the last several years. See Giuseppe Ferraro, "La nuova preghiera di ordinazione presbiterale," *Civiltà Cattolica* 141/3 (1990): 26–39; Pere Tena, "La Prex Ordinationis de los presbíteros en la II edición típica," *Notitiae* 26 (1991): 126–33; Bruno Kleinheyer, "Ordinationsfeiern: Zur zweiten Auflage des Pontifikale-Faszikels 'De Ordinatione Episcopi,

text, the changes are highlighted in boldface type (see Appendix, pp. 108–13). Focusing on the changes is a way to see the key issues and the theological points that needed to be addressed to make the prayer more revelatory of the theology of the Second Vatican Council, particularly of the ecclesiology in the Dogmatic Constitution on the Church, *Lumen gentium*.[19]

The very first section of the prayer, the Prologue invoking God and naming his attributes, introduces several changes. First we find a shift from the language of civic role and duty ("honor and dignity") and the substitution of a theological phrase from The Decree on Religious Freedom, *Dignitatis Humanae*, n. 1: "human dignity." Likewise "progress and stability" are replaced by "graces" (1 Cor 12:4). The major addition in this first section is found in ll. 7-10. God not only organizes the world, the human person, and his graces, but also "forms a priestly people" in his Son Jesus Christ. The trinitarian content of the addition and the placing of orders in a biblical and theological rather than civic vocabulary is an important shift. The language comes from *Lumen gentium*, nn. 10 and 28, and from the Decree on Priestly Life and Ministry, *Presbyterorum Ordinis*, n. 12.

The changes in ll. 12-15 alter the structure somewhat, shifting the section from being a continuation of God's attributes to form-

---

presbyterorum et diaconorum'," *Liturgisches Jahrbuch* 41 (1991): 88–118, esp. 102–8; Salvador Pie, "La plegaria de ordenación de los presbíteros: Nueva edición Ritual," *Phase* 186 (1991): 471–90; Maurice Vidal, "La nouvelle prière d'ordination des prêtres: Réflections théologiques," *La Maison-Dieu* 186 (1991): 23–30; Jan Michael Joncas, "New Roman Rite Prayer of Ordination of Presbyters: A Liturgical Vision of the Priesthood," *Priest* 48/5 (May 1992): 39–47; Joncas, "The Public Language of Minstry Revisited: *De Ordinatione Episcopi, Presbyterorum et Diaconorum* 1990," *Worship* 68 (1994): 386–403, esp. 397–401; Susan K. Wood, "The Liturgical Rite of the Ordination of Presbyters," in *Sacramental Orders*, Lex Orandi Series (Collegeville, MN: Liturgical Press, 2000), 86–116, esp. 97–105.

19. See David N. Power, "Appropriate Ordination Rites: A Historical Perspective," in *Alternative Futures for Worship, Volume 6: Leadership Ministry in Community*, ed. Michael A. Cowan (Collegeville: Liturgical Press, 1987), 131–37, esp. 132.

ing a first anamnesis. Here Moses is identified with governing and Aaron with worship, which will continue in the next two sections. Naming them specifically and eliminating the mention of the Levites clarifies the movement of the prayer.

The change in ll. 26-27 about "the sacrifices of the tabernacle, which were a shadow of the good things to come," touches on the role of OT types in Christian prayers. While valuable for Israel, the People of God, at their own time, for Christians they look forward to Christ who perfects all sacrifice in himself.

The addition of ll. 29-38 provides another trinitarian hymn, focused on Christ's own mission and priesthood (see Heb 3:1-2: "Jesus, the apostle and high priest of our confession, was faithful to the one who appointed him, just as Moses also 'was faithful in all God's house.'"). The priestly image of Christ as spotless victim (Heb 9:14) is combined with the Johannine language of Jesus consecrating the apostles in the truth (John 17:19) and making them sharers in his mission (John 20:21: "As the Father has sent me, so I send you."). The section concludes with a reminiscence of the Constitution on the Liturgy, n. 6: carry the work of salvation throughout the whole world.

The actualization in ll. 39-41 has changed. It is not the weakness of the bishop that requires help, but the rather the nature of the church.

The section that contains the direct epiclesis of the Holy Spirit, the words designated as the essential form by Pius XII, ll. 43-51, have remained unchanged (though newly translated).

The first intercession, ll. 53-57, adds that it is the Holy Spirit that gives the words of preaching their power.

The second intercession, ll. 60-65, is new, as are the words of the third intercession. These intercessions make explicit the work of the priest: celebrating the sacraments (baptism, Eucharist, reconciliation, and anointing of the sick) and praying for the whole world.

The final transition into the doxology, ll. 71-73, gives a clearer eschatological cast to the whole prayer and leads into a final moment of praise and the affirmation of the gathered assembly of the faithful.

Some Theological Reflection

Pere Tena, who gave the official commentary on the prayer in *Notitiae*[20] mentions four particular areas that the revisions attended to in the prayer.

First, the role of priest is presented as an organic collaboration with the order of bishops, and the intercessions clarify the concrete shape that the collaboration takes.

Second, this collaboration is not a concession, for instance, to the bishop's weakness, but a participation in the priesthood of Jesus Christ. This is particularly articulated in the New Testament anamnesis of the prayer.

Third, the prayer's additions attempt to clarify the use of OT typology. In the "earlier covenant," priesthood was exercised in one way, but in Christ it is exercised in another. The sacrifices of the Old Testament are not identical to the sacrifice of New Testament. There is no one-to-one correspondence, and no perfect continuity. All is made new in Christ who fulfills and transforms all that has come before.

Fourth, the theology has been enriched. At three moments, the work of the three persons of the *Trinity* is explicitly raised (the first section, the New Testament anamnesis, and the first intercession). The *ecclesial* context of the action is made more explicit. The initial invocation of God reminds us that he has formed a priestly people. These people (though not again called "priestly") are recalled in the second and third intercessions and the eschatological transition to the doxology. The deepening of the *eschatological* reference just before the doxology also enriches the theology of the prayer, reminding those gathered that all is aiming toward the kingdom, nourished along the way by the Eucharist, the bread for the journey (*viaticum*), that is the last part of the liturgy of ordination.

Concerns

Despite the obvious enrichment of the prayer in the most recent reform, some raise concerns. Most important, while the opening of the prayer mentions the three responsibilities of the priesthood

20. See note 18 above.

of Christ as worship, preaching/teaching, and ruling (priest, prophet, and king), the intercessions seem to omit a prayer for the participation in the governing function. The worship function emerges most strongly, with several references to the preaching/teaching function. Could this be better articulated?

The relationship of the ministerial priesthood and the priesthood of the faithful is touched upon but does not receive any clear expression.

Conclusions

This exploration of the rites of the ordination of priests and the prayer of the ordination of priests has led to a series of individual reflections. At the end, I would like to reflect more globally for a moment. A particular insight of Benedictine theologian Odo Casel touched on the related terms of liturgy as *actio* and liturgy as *participatio*. A student of his, Salvatore Marsili, offered the image of liturgy as "a moment in salvation history." If the celebration of the ordination of priests is an "action" that allows us to "participate" in a moment of salvation history, what might that mean?

The signs that the celebration holds up to us are manifold: call and response, election, immersion in the word of God, prostration in the midst of the saints, receiving the tradition of tasks of service on behalf of the community.

The prayer of ordination inserts us first in the complexities of leadership. There is too much to do. Moses cannot handle all the governing alone. Aaron cannot handle the details of worship alone. They must of necessity share the tasks that are theirs, received from the Lord, with others.

The Lord Jesus from the start calls others to himself. Eventually he sends them forth to continue his ministry, constantly challenging them to be connected to him and to grow forth from him (the vine and the branches).

Today, in the light of how God has acted in the Old Testament and in the New Testament, and transformed by the passion, death, and resurrection of Jesus Christ, the church recognizes its need for companions for the successors of the apostles. The sacrament places in touch with Christ the Head of the church a diversity of ministers: bishops, priests, and deacons, who share in different ways the priesthood (bishops and priests) and ministry of Christ (deacons). This celebration of Christ the Head is one that orders the service of the body of Christ, his members who share his priesthood and who need ordering in order to live out that life of self-offering in Christ that baptism not only implies but demands, that Eucharist actuates in each celebration of the Mass.

To be ordained is to participate in Christ the Head, Christ the Priest, Christ the Teacher, and to exercise that leadership on behalf of the community, priests in collaboration with the bishop.

The sixth-grade boy who was awed by the mystery of the Eucharist and in love with the role of the priest as he understood it as an eleven-year-old has come to know that one must constantly choose: to enter the seminary, to start to pray, to study, to submit to experience of faithful guides, to set out in new directions. And always to reengage with life, with love, with friends, with God, with liturgy. To choose priesthood at eleven, to decide to ask for ordination at twenty-five, to still be a priest at fifty-eight—this a part of a process of constant choice to allow Christ to be head, to allow the liturgy to draw me into the mystery of his dying and rising, and to be open to the transformation constantly demanded of me.

The idealized image of a childhood priest, the teaching and example of seminary faculty, the transformation of ordination, the living of service on behalf of the community in the person of Christ the head and how it has forced me constantly to choose anew to be that servant—all this is mine as I reflect on ordination in the Year for Priests.

Chapter 4

Priesthood, Priestliness, and Priests

Monsignor Paul G. McPartlan

The year we are currently celebrating is called the "Year for Priests" in English, or the "Year of the Priest," and similarly in German, *das Jahr des Priesters or das Priester-Jahr*. In Latin, French, Italian, and Spanish, however, it's the "Priestly Year": *Annus sacerdotalis, Année sacerdotale, Anno sacerdotale, Año sacerdotal*. This is rather curious, since priestliness actually goes wider than just the *priests* who are clearly the focus of the year. The first letter of Peter teaches that the whole church is "a chosen race, a royal priesthood" (1 Pet 2:9), and the Second Vatican Council took this up in its Dogmatic Constitution on the Church, *Lumen Gentium*: "the baptized, by regeneration and the anointing of the Holy Spirit, are consecrated to be a spiritual house and a holy priesthood."[1] So the whole people of God is a priestly people.

Then again, those whom we commonly call "priests" were normally called *presbyters* (*presbyteri*) by the council, reviving an early Christian word for the bishop's council of elders, and the council invited us to think first of the bishop himself when we consider ministerial priesthood; it is he who has the fulness of

---

1. *Lumen Gentium* (LG) 10. Vatican II quotations are taken from Austin Flannery, ed., *Vatican Council II*, vol. 1, *The Conciliar and Post Conciliar Documents*, new revised ed. (New York/Dublin: Costello Publishing Company/Dominican Publications, 1996). Scripture quotations are from the New Revised Standard Version.

61

orders, the high priesthood.[2] Strictly speaking, then, it could be said that a Year for Priests should have us thinking first of all of bishops and then of those who are ordained to be their cowork-ers, or *cooperatores* as the council says, namely, the presbyters.[3] Certainly it raises the question again as to the relationship be-tween bishops and priests. One bishop I know will happily con-celebrate with a priest presiding, while another I can think of will always preside.

Perhaps it is providential that this year has its different names, because that invites us to ponder more fully the nuances of the terms: priesthood, priestliness, and priests, and to appreciate more deeply the mystery of the church and the interrelatedness of all its members in their respective callings. There are undoubt-edly complexities here, but let us grasp the challenge.

An Ordered Community

This is one of the areas of church theology and practice where it is most necessary to have recourse to history and to learn from it. How did we get to where we are? I would like to start with what might be called a fundamental theology of ordination. St. Paul instructed the unruly Corinthians that everything should be done "decently and in order (*kata taxin*)" (1 Cor 14:40). This doesn't seem to be an instruction about tidiness but about behav-ing in accordance with one's true gifts in a properly ordered community. Earlier on, he had indicated some of the different offices in the church, the body of Christ, that came from God's appointment: "first apostles, second prophets, third teachers; then deeds of power, then gifts of healing, forms of assistance, forms of leadership, various kinds of tongues." "Are all apostles?" he said. "Are all prophets? Are all teachers? Do all work miracles? Do all possess gifts of healing? Do all speak in tongues? Do all interpret?" (1 Cor 12:28-30). His point is that there are different callings or ranks or *orders* in the church, and each must know his or her proper place and role, and fulfil it, for the benefit of all.

2. Cf. LG 21.
3. Cf. LG 28; also *Presbyterorum Ordinis* (PO) 2, 4.

The church is an ordered community, and, as the *Catechism of the Catholic Church* teaches, since ancient times the church has recognised various orders, such as the order of bishops (*ordo episcoporum*), the order of presbyters, the order of deacons, and others, too: the orders of catechumens, virgins, spouses, widows,[4] and we might add the order of penitents, too. Strictly speaking, as it adds, integration into any of these bodies in the church was an *ordinatio*, or ordination. So, "ordination" is actually a word like "graduation," it requires further specification: Which degree or stage of education? Which order? The *Catechism* notes that, over the course of time, "ordination" has in fact become "reserved for the sacramental act which integrates a man into the order of bishops, presbyters, or deacons,"[5] but that should not blind us to the existence of other orders still today. We might note that John Zizioulas and other Orthodox theologians would urge us to see chrismation or confirmation as ordination into the rank of layperson in the church.[6]

Zizioulas also notes that St. Paul alludes to the liturgical action of the Eucharist when he says, again to the Corinthians: "For in him [Christ] every one of God's promises is a 'Yes.' For this reason it is through him that we say the 'Amen,' to the glory of God" (2 Cor 1:20).[7] The picture is one of Christ, fully open to his Father in a "Yes" that humanity otherwise has never managed, and all the faithful finding their own access to the Father through him, with him, and in him, with a great "Amen" that participates in his own "Yes"; and Paul's statement obviously presupposes a basic distinction within the community between "those who lead the Eucharistic community by offering the Eucharist and those who confirm or seal this action with their 'Amen,'"[8] or, more

---

4. Cf. *Catechism of the Catholic Church*, with modifications from the *Editio Typica* (Washington, DC: USCCB, 1997), hereafter CCC, n. 1537.

5. CCC 1538.

6. Cf. John Zizioulas, *Being as Communion* (London: Darton, Longman & Todd, 1985), p. 153.

7. Cf. *Being as Communion*, p. 121.

8. John Zizioulas, "The Early Christian Community," in Bernard McGinn, John Meyendorff, Jean Leclerq, eds., *Christian Spirituality: Origins to the*

specifically, between those who represent to the community Christ himself, saying his "Yes," and those who respond with the "Amen" it evokes. Zizioulas is insistent that the Amen "always formed an integral and indispensable part of the Eucharist" and that it was the exclusive prerogative of the laity to utter it.[9]

As is well known, priestly language is used with only two referents in the New Testament, namely Christ himself and the Christian people. The letter to the Hebrews is the great source for understanding Christ the priest, or rather the High Priest (cf. Heb 5:5-10; 8:1; 9:11-12), as it repeatedly calls him, who has made his one single sacrifice for sins by offering himself and then taken his place forever at the right hand of God (cf. Heb 10:12). In fact, the letter invites us to understand Christ as priestly all through his life. "In the days of his flesh," it says, "Jesus offered up prayers and supplications, with loud cries and tears, to the one who was able to save him from death" (Heb 5:7). That is how we are to think of him at all times, pouring out his heart to his Father in a total priestly offering, which simply culminated on the cross. Moreover, the letter directs us to understand Jesus as priestly still today: "he holds his priesthood permanently," it says. "Consequently he is able for all time to save those who approach God through him, since he always lives to make intercession for them" (Heb 7:24-25). That is how we have access to the Father. Christ is the channel, the intercessor, forever saying his "Yes"!

It follows that just as Christ is by his very nature priestly, so anyone who is "in Christ" by baptism is also priestly. There is no way to participate in Christ without being caught up in his own movement to his Father, giving his all, and Sts. Peter and Paul unite in telling us that we ourselves are to bring something into that very movement, namely "spiritual sacrifices," the offering

---

Twelfth Century (London: Routledge and Kegan Paul, 1986), pp. 23–43, here at 30.

9. Cf. John Zizioulas, "The Theological Problem of 'Reception,'" *One in Christ* 21 (1985), pp. 187–193, here at 192; also Paul McPartlan, *The Eucharist Makes the Church: Henri de Lubac and John Zizioulas in Dialogue*, 2nd ed. (Fairfax, VA: Eastern Christian Publications, 2006; first published, 1993), p. 196.

of our selves. "Come to him," says the first letter of Peter, "a living stone, though rejected by mortals yet chosen and precious in God's sight; and like living stones, let yourselves be built into a spiritual house, to be a holy priesthood, to offer spiritual sacrifices acceptable to God through Jesus Christ" (1 Pet 2:4-5). Paul says to the Romans: "I appeal to you therefore, brothers and sisters, by the mercies of God, to present your bodies as a living sacrifice, holy and acceptable to God, which is your spiritual worship [*logiké latreía*]" (Rom 12:1). But how are we to "come to him" and offer the sacrifice of ourselves to be taken up in his own once and for all offering? How can this essential dynamic of the Christian life be activated and become a lived reality that focuses our lives and energises us as it ought? Only by being regularly enacted in the sacred drama that we call *liturgy*, and the liturgical act *par excellence* in which it is realised is the Eucharist.

In his apostolic exhortation, *Sacramentum Caritatis*, Pope Benedict calls on St. Augustine (354–430) as he explains this mystery:

> Here the eucharistic celebration appears in all its power as the source and summit of the Church's life, since it expresses at once both the origin and the fulfilment of the new and definitive worship of God, the *logiké latreía*. St Paul's exhortation to the Romans in this regard is a concise description of how the Eucharist makes our whole life a spiritual worship pleasing to God. . . . The bishop of Hippo goes on to say that: "this is the sacrifice of Christians: that we, though many, are one body in Christ. The Church celebrates this mystery in the sacrament of the altar, as the faithful know, and there she shows them clearly that in what is offered, she herself is offered."[10]

In a fine sentence from its first agreed statement on "Eucharistic Doctrine" (1971), the international Anglican-Roman Catholic dialogue said that in the eucharistic prayer, the members of Christ "entreat the benefits of his passion on behalf of the whole Church,

---

10. Pope Benedict XVI, Apostolic Exhortation, *Sacramentum Caritatis* (2007), n. 70, quotation from St. Augustine, *De civitate Dei* 10, 6 (PL 41, 284).

participate in those benefits and enter into the movement of his self-offering."[11]

By the very nature of what is happening, such a liturgy must have a presider who represents Christ the head of the body in his once and for all sacrifice and receives the gifts of the members of the body that are to be taken up into that sacrifice. It needs someone who will represent Christ *to* the community, so that they can actually enact their response to him, offering themselves symbolically in the gifts of bread and wine that are brought up and placed on the altar. That is exactly how the *Catechism* describes the ordained: "In the ecclesial service of the ordained minister, it is Christ himself who is present to his Church as Head of his Body, Shepherd of his flock, high priest of the redemptive sacrifice, Teacher of Truth."[12] Our membership of the body of Christ and our calling in that capacity to offer spiritual sacrifices through him, with him, and in him are made real for us liturgically and sacramentally, whereby we enact in earthly forms things divine. Sacramentally configured to Christ by ordination, the presider represents him offering his once and for all sacrifice, and the bread and wine become his body and blood, sacramentally given to his members.

Priests of the New Covenant

We need those sacred symbols. I am always struck by the wisdom of a little phrase used by the Council of Trent in its teaching on the sacrifice of the Mass. It says that Christ, who was once and for all to offer himself to God the Father on the cross, left his church a visible sacrifice "as human nature requires [*sicut hominum natura exigit*]" by which his one bloody sacrifice might be present and its power applied until the end of the world.[13] Human nature does require that the all-important mysteries now invisible

---

11. Anglican-Roman Catholic International Commission (ARCIC), agreed statement, "Eucharistic Doctrine" (1971), n. 5; in *The Final Report* (London: CTS/SPCK, 1982), p. 14.

12. CCC 1548, cf. *Sacramentum Caritatis* 23.

13. See next note.

to us be made visible and accessible so that we can engage with them as flesh-and-blood historical beings here and now. That is what the sacraments are for.

The phrase occurs in the immensely long sentence which ends with Trent's crucial affirmation that Jesus entrusted this visible sacrifice to the apostles at the Last Supper and constituted them as "priests of the New Covenant." We need to see the carefully crafted sentence in full. It is broken into a short sentence and then a long one in the following translation, and it is worth noting among other things that, with repeated references to the letter to the Hebrews, Trent offers strong reassurance here against Protestant fears that Catholics *repeat* the sacrifice of Christ in the Mass.

> He, then, our Lord and God, was once and for all to offer himself to God the Father by his death on the altar of the cross (cf. Heb 7:27), to accomplish for them an everlasting redemption. Because, however, his priesthood was not to end with his death (cf. Heb 7:24), at the Last Supper, "on the night when he was betrayed" (1 Cor 11:23), in order to leave his beloved Spouse the Church a visible sacrifice (as human nature requires), by which the bloody sacrifice which he was once and for all to accomplish on the cross would be present, its memory perpetuated until the end of the world and its salutary power applied for the forgiveness of sins which we daily commit; declaring himself constituted "a priest for ever after the order of Melchizedek" (Ps 109:4; Heb 5:6; 7:17), he offered his body and blood under the species of bread and wine to God the Father, and, under the same signs gave them to partake of to the Apostles (whom he then established as priests of the New Covenant [*Novi Testamenti sacerdotes*]), and ordered them and their successors in the priesthood to offer, saying: "Do this in memory of me" (Lk 22:19; 1 Cor 11:24), etc., as the Catholic Church has always understood and taught.[14]

---

14. Council of Trent, Doctrine and Canons on the Sacrifice of the Mass, 17 September 1562, chapter one (DS 1740); cf. J. Neuner, J. Dupuis, eds., *The Christian Faith in the Doctrinal Documents of the Catholic Church*, 7th ed. (New York: Alba House 2001), p. 627 (amended translation).

Lots of ecumenical issues arise with regard to this Catholic teaching that Christ constituted the twelve apostles as priests when he instituted the sacrament of the Eucharist at the Last Supper (thereby also instituting the sacrament of ordination), a teaching reiterated in the *Catechism*.[15] Many have disputed the evidence for it. In response, the former dean of the School of Theology and Religious Studies here at CUA, Francis Moloney, rather disarmingly once acknowledged that "there is no literary or historical evidence for this tradition." However, he then hit the nail on the head by saying: "The Catholic tradition has caught the *symbolic importance* of the relationship between the Eucharist and the priesthood."[16] That is nicely put. It is obvious that Jesus did not lay his hands on the apostles at the Last Supper and say: I now ordain you as priests. What he was doing, however, was instituting the sacrament, namely the Eucharist, which was to sustain his followers through the years to come by giving them access to his own enduring sacrifice, and instructing the founding leaders of the church, the apostles, to continue that action: "Do this in memory of me." And the fact is that, under the guidance of the Holy Spirit,[17] those who were appointed to lead the church in the years that followed and to preside at the Eucharist (the two tasks consistently went together as Hervé-Marie Legrand has shown[18]), were increasingly understood to be not just successors of the apostles in their leadership but representatives of Christ to his people in the eucharistic celebration, and therefore priestly, because he is the High Priest.

In other words, a great deal of doctrinal development is telescoped by the Council of Trent in its affirmation that Christ es-

---

15. Cf. CCC 1337.

16. Francis Moloney, "The Catholic Priesthood: A New Testament Reflection," *New Theology Review* (August 2004), pp. 5–18, here at 10 (emphasis in original).

17. The promise of Jesus to his disciples, significantly given at the Last Supper, namely that the Holy Spirit "will guide you into all the truth" (John 16:13) must be remembered here.

18. Cf. Hervé-Marie Legrand, "The Presidency of the Eucharist according to the Ancient Tradition," in Kevin Seasoltz, ed., *Living Bread, Saving Cup* (Collegeville: Liturgical Press, 1987), pp. 196–221.

tablished the apostles as priests at the Last Supper. It may be helpful to our brothers and sisters in other Christian traditions for us Catholics to say that we mean he *implicitly* established them as priests on that occasion, and thereby implicitly instituted the sacrament of ordination too. The phrasing of Trent may not be ideal, but the insight it captures is crucial. The institution of the Eucharist must have been the institution of the ministerial priesthood also, even though it took the church some years to think that through.

Moloney is quite correct, then, to highlight the symbolic importance of the relationship between the Eucharist and the priesthood that is perceived in the Catholic tradition, but I think there is more to be said. There is a further relationship that the Catholic tradition perceives, and that is between Eucharist and *apostolicity*. It is completely appropriate that the apostles, the Twelve, who are the foundations of the church, should be entrusted with the Eucharist, because in the famous phrase of Henri de Lubac (1896–1991), "the Eucharist makes the Church."[19] To preside at the Eucharist is not just a priestly act, imaging Christ the priest, it is also an apostolic act because the Eucharist builds up the church that is founded on the apostles, to use the imagery of the book of Revelation (cf. Rev 21:9-14). I think it needs to be added, therefore, that the Catholic tradition catches the symbolic importance of the link between the Eucharist and the apostles,[20] and therefore between priesthood and the apostles, and that also is why the Catholic Church teaches so firmly that the priesthood of the New Covenant was essentially instituted at the Last Supper and conferred by Christ on the twelve apostles.

It is worth noting that "priests of the New Covenant," to use Trent's phrase, are very different from priests of the Old Covenant. Strictly speaking, there is only one priest of the New Covenant, and that is Christ himself; and priests of the New Covenant,

---

19. Henri de Lubac, *Corpus Mysticum*, trans. Gemma Simmonds (London: SCM, 2006), p. 88; cf. McPartlan, *The Eucharist Makes the Church*.

20. Cf. Pope John Paul II, Encyclical Letter, *Ecclesia de Eucharistia*, 2003, chapter three, titled "The Apostolicity of the Eucharist and of the Church," nn. 26–33.

in the plural, are simply those who are sacramentally configured to him so as to represent him and his priesthood in the church's liturgical actions. He is the focal point; he is the priest. All who are baptised into him are priestly and are called to offer themselves in his self-offering, and so that that mystery can actually be put into practice some of the baptised are appointed to preside and represent Christ the head, Christ the priest, to his members, making his sacrifice present in their midst and receiving their priestly sacrifices to be united with his. The whole church therefore *inhabits* his one sacrifice, so to speak. To understand priests of the New Covenant aright, we must start with Christ, and then consider the priestly people, and then finally consider the ministerial priests in their midst who make Christ and his sacrifice present to his own, as the essential reference point for their whole lives. That is the sequence of understanding that Vatican II follows in LG 10, with its account of the two distinct sharings in the one priesthood of Christ that the faithful and the ordained respectively have, and it is heartening to see the same order again in the most significant ecumenical statement achieved since Vatican II, namely the 1982 Lima Report of the Faith and Order Commission of the World Council of Churches, titled *Baptism, Eucharist and Ministry*, which also remarkably affirms that the ordained "may appropriately be called priests because they fulfil a particular priestly service by strengthening and building up the royal and prophetic priesthood of the faithful."[21] Long ago, St. Augustine put it succinctly when he said to his people, "with you I am a Christian, for you I am a bishop [*vobis sum episcopus, vobiscum christianus*]."[22]

A Glance at History

Which brings us back to bishops again, and the need for a glance at history. We do not know who presided at the Eucharist in New Testament times, except for Paul at Troas in Acts 20:7-12,

---

21. *Baptism, Eucharist and Ministry* (Faith and Order Paper no. 111; Geneva: World Council of Churches, 1982), "Ministry," 17.
22. Augustine, *Sermo* 340, 1 (PL 38, 1483).

but we do know that the life of the NT church was intensely eucharistic. John Paul Heil has explained how the letters of St. Paul
are best understood through a eucharistic lens,[23] and Denis
Farkasfalvy has convincingly shown that "the narrative tradition
that stands behind the Synoptics was formed and shaped in [the]
'eucharistic cradle' of early Christian liturgy."[24] It seems reasonable to assume that the elders (*presbyteroi*) or overseers (*episkopoi*)
of the early communities presided at the liturgy. *Presbyteroi* and
episkopoi seem to have been interchangeable terms, and we find
these terms in the plural, indicating a corporate leadership, rather
like that in the Jewish synagogues.[25] It is with St. Ignatius of
Antioch (c. 35–c. 107), in the letters he wrote on his way to Rome
to be martyred, that we first find the terms differentiated and a
new configuration emerging, whereby there is one *episkopos* in
each place, surrounded by a *presbyterium*, a body of *presbyteroi*.

Ignatius urges the local communities that he writes to on his
way to martyrdom in Rome to be united with their bishop especially for the celebration of the Eucharist. In a well-known quote,
he says: "Wherever the bishop is to be seen, there let all the
people be, just as wherever Jesus Christ is, there is the catholic
church."[26] He sees the bishop as imaging Christ or God himself,
and the presbyters that surround him imaging the apostles, to
whom Jesus said in the gospel: "when the Son of man is seated
on the throne of his glory, you who have followed me will also
sit on twelve thrones, judging the twelve tribes of Israel" (Matt
19:28; cf. Luke 22:30).[27] It seems, therefore, that the lived experience of the liturgy as a foretaste of the kingdom of God and of

23. Cf. John Paul Heil, "Theology and Worship in the Later Letters of
Paul," unpublished paper, delivered at a Pauline Symposium held at The
Catholic University of America, 20 March 2009.

24. Denis Farkasfalvy, "The Eucharistic Provenance of New Testament
Texts," in Roch A. Kereszty, ed., *Rediscovering the Eucharist: Ecumenical Conversations* (New York/Mahwah: Paulist, 2003), pp. 27–51, here at 34.

25. Cf. Raymond E. Brown, "*Episkopé* and *Episkopos*: The New Testament
Evidence," *Theological Studies* 41 (1980), pp. 322–38, here at 327.

26. Ignatius of Antioch, *Smyrnaeans*, 8. This is the first time that the expression "catholic church" appears in Christian literature.

27. Cf. Ignatius of Antioch, *Magnesians*, 6; *Trallians*, 3.

judgement day itself, scenes in which there is one central figure, namely Christ, gradually led to the singling out of one leader of the community in its worship, namely the bishop, who imaged Christ in the liturgy, surrounded by the presbyters who imaged the apostles.

There is something slightly awkward here in that christological and apostolic imagery are split between the bishop and the presbyters, respectively. However, a century or so later, in the so-called *Apostolic Tradition*, we find christological and apostolic imagery firmly united in the person of the bishop. The *Apostolic Tradition* is a complex and multilayered work, commonly associated with Hippolytus (c. 170–c. 236), but in fact many times revised, though it possibly does originate in third-century Rome.[28] This work was thought to be lost for many centuries until it was identified again early in the twentieth-century, causing great excitement across the different Christian traditions. The *Apostolic Tradition* duly had a major impact on Vatican II, and provided Eucharistic Prayer II for the revised *Roman Missal* (1970), among other things.

The ordination prayers in the *Apostolic Tradition* give us precious insights into the roles of bishop, presbyter, and deacon in the early church. The prayer for the ordination of a bishop asks God to "pour forth that power which is from you, of the spirit of leadership that you gave to your beloved Son Jesus Christ [there is the christological link], which he gave to the holy apostles [there is the apostolic link], who established the Church in every place." It continues: "Bestow, knower of the heart, Father, on this your servant, whom you have chosen for the episcopate, to feed your holy flock and to exercise the high priesthood for you without blame, ministering night and day; unceasingly to propitiate your countenance, and to offer to you the holy gifts of your church."[29] The bishop is therefore to lead his people and to pre-

---

28. Cf. John F. Baldovin, "Hippolytus and the Apostolic Tradition: Recent Research and Commentary," *Theological Studies* 64 (2003), 520–42.

29. *Apostolic Tradition*, §3, 3-4, in Paul F. Bradshaw, Maxwell E. Johnson, L. Edward Phillips, *The Apostolic Tradition* (Minneapolis: Fortress Press, 2002), p. 30.

side at the Eucharist, offering the gifts and feeding the flock, exercising the "high priesthood." It is important to note that the bishop's high priesthood is not in reference to the presbyters' *priesthood*. No priesthood at all is explicitly attributed to the presbyters; their ordination prayer simply asks God for "the spirit of grace and of counsel of the presbyterate" so that those ordained "may help and govern your people with a pure heart."[30] The presbyters were the bishop's council, who advised him in the governance of the church. He alone presided at the liturgy, and his "high priesthood" echoes the title given to Christ in the letter to the Hebrews, and so constitutes another christological reference. Nevertheless, the presbyters extended their hands with those of the bishop over the gifts in the liturgy,[31] and there is a hint that in some sense they are priestly later in the *Apostolic Tradition* when the ordination of a deacon is described. On that occasion, it says, only the bishop is to lay on hands "because he [the deacon] is not ordained to the priesthood but to the service of the bishop."[32] If the deacon is not ordained to the priesthood, the implication is that the presbyter in some sense *is* so ordained, presumably sharing in the priesthood of the bishop, but the reference is rather elusive.[33]

Among the early fathers, then, the title "high priest" or simply "priest" referred to the bishop.[34] This changed in the fourth century, when the whole situation of the church changed and Christianity was first tolerated under Constantine and then embraced as the religion of the Roman Empire under Theodosius. The number of Christians increased dramatically and it was no longer possible for all the Christians to meet with their bishop for the Sunday Eucharist. The eventual solution was the formation of

---

30. *Apostolic Tradition*, §7, 2, in Bradshaw, et al., *The Apostolic Tradition*, p. 56.

31. Cf. *Apostolic Tradition*, §4, 2, in Bradshaw et al., *The Apostolic Tradition*, p. 38.

32. *Apostolic Tradition*, §8, 2, in Bradshaw et al., *The Apostolic Tradition*, p. 60.

33. Cf. Bradshaw et al., *The Apostolic Tradition*, p. 65.

34. See also, e.g., Cyprian, *Letter* 57, 3, 2, and *Letter* 63, 14, 3.

parishes by the subdivision of dioceses, and the break up of the presbyterium so that the presbyters could take charge of the parishes, one in each place. In their parishes, they would now regularly preside at the liturgy, and the ordination prayer for a presbyter evolved at this time so as to consecrate him for a priestly role. This is when the parish priest first appears. Various practices kept alive the sense that the parish Eucharist was an extension of the bishop's Eucharist and that he was still really the presider at the Eucharist of his entire local church, practices such as the *fermentum*, the bringing of a fragment of the bishop's Eucharist to be mingled with the elements on the altar in the parish, but the fact is that slowly but surely over the coming centuries the bishop gradually ceased to be evident as a eucharistic presider and actually became a manager of eucharistic communities.

This was a momentous change. The Orthodox theologian Alexander Schmemann said that the rise of the parish, and the shift of the bishop from eucharistic president to administrator of parishes, "represents one of the most radical changes that ever took place in the Church."[35] Zizioulas considers that "by giving the presbyter the functions which belonged originally to the bishop, the Church turned him into a bishop, and thus lost the presbyter." But more serious was the danger of losing the *bishop*. Zizioulas argues that "we are still wrestling" ecumenically with the consequences of this shift,[36] because a bishop cut off from the Eucharist, a bishop who was just an administrator, was in danger of becoming a rather worldly figure and being considered superfluous to the needs of the church. In the fulness of time the Reformers in many places, though not all, duly abolished bishops, with the result that ecumenical discussion of ordained ministry today has to reckon with the fact that not all Christian traditions

35. Alexander Schmemann, "Towards a Theology of Councils," *St. Vladimir's Seminary Quarterly* 6 (1962), pp. 170–84, here at 177.

36. John D. Zizioulas, "Episkopé and Episkopos in the Early Church: A Brief Survey of the Evidence," in *Episkopé and episkopate in ecumenical perspective* (Faith and Order paper n. 102; Geneva: World Council of Churches, 1980), pp. 30–42, here at 38–39.

still maintain the ancient threefold ministry of bishop, presbyter, and deacon.[37] "The Reformation drew the right conclusions from the fourth century," says Zizioulas, "and quite significantly it found support in Jerome in order to abolish episcopacy."[38] St. Jerome (c. 345–420), writing in the fourth and early fifth century, maintained that, since bishops and presbyters could both consecrate the body and blood of Christ, they were clearly the same in terms of priesthood. As David Power says: "according to Jerome the distinction in authority between bishop and presbyter is a matter of Church custom, and there is no distinction at all in priesthood."[39] Importantly, Jerome still maintained that bishops were the successors of the apostles, vital for the unity of the church, and that only they should ordain,[40] but once again we note that apostolic and christological imagery have diverged; now the bishop is apostolic in his authority and the presbyters are christological in their priesthood, with regard to which the bishop is their equal.

These views had a strong influence centuries later on scholastic theology. St. Thomas Aquinas (c. 1225–1274) said something of perennial importance when he taught: "the sacrament of Order is directed to the sacrament of the Eucharist, which is the sacrament of sacraments."[41] He too captures that link between Eucharist and order that we have already seen. However, for him, as generally for the scholastics, following the eucharistic controversies of the eleventh century in particular, "Eucharist" primarily meant the transformation of bread and wine into the body and blood of Christ by transubstantiation. Priests could do that, and becoming a bishop added nothing to that power, so Aquinas' account of the seven ranks of holy orders culminated in the priest.

---

37. Here, again, it is notable that the Lima Report states that "the threefold ministry of bishop, presbyter and deacon may serve today as an expression of the unity we seek and also as a means for achieving it" (*Baptism, Eucharist and Ministry*, "Ministry," 22).

38. Zizioulas, "Episkopé and Episkopos in the Early Church," p. 39.

39. David N. Power, *Ministers of Christ and His Church: A Theology of the Priesthood* (London: Geoffrey Chapman, 1969), p. 80.

40. Cf. Power, *Ministers of Christ and His Church*, pp. 80–81.

41. Thomas Aquinas, *Summa Theologiae*, Suppl., q. 37, art. 2, resp.

The priest had "the fulness of orders," so to speak, though he did not use that expression. The episcopate was not part of the sacrament of Orders. The bishop was distinguished from the priest not in power of order but in power of jurisdiction;[42] his episcopal consecration gave him power over Christ's mystical body, the church.[43] Yves Congar laments the transition at this time from an ecclesiology of communion to what he calls "an ecclesiology of powers,"[44] and we might note that implicit in this framing of doctrine is a separation between the Eucharist and the church. The priest had full power of order to confect the Eucharist, and the bishop had power of jurisdiction over the church, but the confection of the Eucharist and the government of the church were now in two distinct compartments. As de Lubac notes, the fact that the Eucharist makes the church was now being seriously neglected.[45]

There are some anomalies in this framework. In particular, if the priest has power to celebrate the Eucharist, and the Eucharist is "the sacrament of sacraments," why can the priest not celebrate all of the sacraments? Why are confirmation and ordination performed only by the bishop? Many of the scholastics believed that priests did receive the power to ordain at their own priestly ordination, but that only a bishop had authority to exercise the power. David Power draws attention to Guerric of St. Quentin (died 1245), who believed that priests did have the power to ordain but that they should exercise it "only in case of necessity and then without solemnity, because only a bishop can ordain with solemnity."[46] My parish priest in London believed exactly

---

42. Cf. Laurent Villemin, *Pouvoir d'ordre et pouvoir de juridiction: histoire théologique de leur distinction* (Paris: Cerf, 2003).

43. Cf. Aquinas, *Summa Theologiae*, Suppl., q. 38, art. 2, resp. 2.

44. Yves M.-J. Congar, "L'«Ecclesia» ou communauté chrétienne, sujet intégral de l'action liturgique," in J.-P. Jossua, Y. Congar, eds., *La liturgie après Vatican II* (Paris: Cerf, 1967), pp. 241–82, here at 261.

45. Cf. Henri de Lubac, *Corpus Mysticum*, pp. 114, 162, 256–62.

46. Power, *Ministers of Christ and His Church*, p. 117. In his *Quaestio de ordine*, Guerric says: "Dispositio ad collationem ordinis est sacerdotium, forma vero est auctoritas Ecclesiae, quam habet episcopus. Quae forma potest venire supra materiam aut cum solemnitate, sicut cum episcopus ordinat, aut sine

the same thing; he had learnt it from his own theological formation in the 1940s, and he used to tease periodically the bishop
who lived with us in the presbytery by saying that of course he
himself could ordain if necessary!

Very interestingly, that conviction, held by the scholastics and
often debated within Catholic theology, was also held by certain
Anglicans in the seventeenth and eighteenth centuries, with
major ecumenical consequences for today. John Wesley (1703–
1791), the founder of Methodism, read studies of the early church
by Lord Peter King (1669–1734) and Bishop Edward Stillingfleet
(1635–1699) in the 1740s, and these convinced him that, as he
wrote: "bishops and presbyters are the same order, and consequently have the same right to ordain."[47] In due course, in 1784,
Wesley, an Anglican priest, mightily concerned about how to
provide for the 15,000 or so Methodists in North America, "set
apart" or "ordained" Thomas Coke (1747–1814), another Anglican priest, as "Superintendent," and sent him across the Atlantic
with a new ordinal and the solemn charge to ordain Francis
Asbury (1745–1816) when he arrived. Asbury, a layman, was duly
ordained deacon, elder, and superintendent on three successive
days and joined Coke in charge of "the brethren in North
America." Though he was rebuked by Wesley for doing so,
Asbury subsequently used the title "Bishop,"[48] and the rest is
history. As a faithful Anglican, Wesley believed that though a
priest could ordain only a bishop had the authority generally to
do so. Nevertheless, giving a further twist to the fascinating tale,

---

solemnitate, ubi est necessitas. Sed si non sit necessitas non debet sine
solemnitate venire, et ideo simplex sacerdos non potest ordinare sine neces-
sitate dispensante" (q. 7, resp.; quoted from Augustine McDevitt, "The Episcopate as an Order and Sacrament on the Eve of the High Scholastic Period,"
Franciscan Studies 20 [1960], pp. 96–148, here at 144). It would seem, then,
that "solemnity" refers to the formal authority of the act rather than just the
"trappings."

47. John Wesley, *Letters* vii, 238; quoted in A. Raymond George, "Ordination," in Rupert Davies, A. Raymond George, Gordon Rupp, eds., *History of
the Methodist Church in Great Britain*, vol. 2 (London: Epworth, 1978), pp.
143–60, here at 148.

48. Cf. A. Raymond George, "Ordination," pp. 145–47.

he believed that since he himself had charge of the whole Methodist flock by the will of God, although unconsecrated he was *de facto*, as he said, "as real a Christian bishop as the Archbishop of Canterbury."[49]

Returning to consideration of the Catholic fold, we may note that there were anomalies, too, in the teaching of Trent, which said that "the power of consecrating, offering and administering [Christ's] body and blood . . . was given to the apostles and to their successors in the priesthood [*in sacerdotio*]," but then later spoke of the importance of the hierarchy in the ordering of the church, and of the principal place in the hierarchy occupied by "the bishops, who have succeeded the apostles."[50] Who, then, we might ask, are the successors of the apostles: the priests who offer the Eucharist or the bishops who govern the church? Clearly both have a good claim, and the conundrum arises because of the separation between the Eucharist and the church.

The Teaching of Vatican II

The conundrum was resolved by Vatican II: the bishops are the successors of the apostles, and the responsibility for celebrating the Eucharist in the church rests primarily with them.[51] The council benefited greatly from the biblical, patristic, and liturgical renewal of the previous decades. One of the most significant developments in twentieth-century Catholic and Orthodox ecclesiology was the revival of eucharistic ecclesiology, an appreciation of the ecclesial dimension of the Eucharist and

49. Wesley, *Letters* vii, 162; quoted in A. Raymond George, "Ordination," p. 147; cf. pp. 148–50. Though Wesley drew his understanding predominantly from the early church, via the works of King and Stillingfleet, and was not influenced by scholasticism, the similarity between his viewpoint and that of Guerric, who believed that for the conferring of orders the authority of the church, "ordinarily supplied solemnly by the episcopal consecration," but sometimes supplied "by necessity" (McDevitt, "Episcopate," p. 121), is remarkable. Wesley believed that in the necessity of his times he had effectively been consecrated.

50. Council of Trent, Doctrine on the Sacrament of Order, 1563, chapter one, DS 1764, and chapter four, DS 1768, respectively.

51. Cf. LG 22 and 26, respectively.

of the eucharistic dimension of the church that can be summarised in the principle: the Eucharist makes the church.[52] St. Augustine is perhaps most associated with this understanding in the West; we receive the body of Christ and so become the body of Christ: "be what you see," he said, "and receive what you are."[53] *Lumen Gentium* quoted St. Leo the Great (died 461) in a similar vein: "the sharing in the body and blood of Christ has no other effect than to accomplish our transformation into that which we receive."[54] The council taught that the eucharistic sacrifice is "the source and summit of the Christian life,"[55] and we might also recall the title of Pope John Paul's final encyclical: *Ecclesia de Eucharistia* (2003).

Within this perspective it becomes possible to integrate two very important teachings of scholastic theology that had long remained rather disconnected: first of all, that the sacrament of ordination is directed to the sacrament of the Eucharist; and second, that the bishop's responsibility is to govern and care for the church. If the building up of the church is now appreciated as the fulness of the meaning of the Eucharist, then it becomes possible to appreciate the episcopacy itself as the fulness of the sacrament of order, and that is what Vatican II did in LG 21, calling episcopacy once again the "high priesthood," with reference to the *Apostolic Tradition*. It follows that the bishop leads his diocese, or rather his local church, from behind the altar rather than from behind a desk. The very priestly prayer for ordaining a bishop in the *Apostolic Tradition* was reinstated after Vatican II,[56]

52. See above, note 19. Also, Paul McPartlan, *Sacrament of Salvation: An Introduction to Eucharistic Ecclesiology* (Edinburgh: T & T Clark, 1995); Walter Cardinal Kasper, *Sacrament of Unity: The Eucharist and the Church* (New York: Crossroad, 2004).

53. "*Estote quod videtis, et accipite quod estis*"; Augustine, *Sermo* 272 (PL 38: 1247–1248).

54. Leo, *Sermo* 63 (PL 54: 357C), quoted in LG 26.

55. LG 11.

56. Cf. Bernard Botte, *From Silence to Participation: An Insider's View of Liturgical Renewal*, trans. John Sullivan (Washington, DC: The Pastoral Press, 1988), pp. 133–35.

with the firm understanding that a bishop is indeed "ordained" and not just "consecrated."

After LG 21 comes LG 22, and LG 22 contains Vatican II's famous teaching on episcopal collegiality. Kenan Osborne perceptively remarks that when power of order and power of jurisdiction were distinguished that necessarily affected the basis of collegiality. All scholastics believed that the college of bishops succeeded the college of the apostles, but the basis of that collegial responsibility was the power of jurisdiction received from the pope, and from early in the second millennium collegial activity became restricted to ecumenical councils summoned by the pope.[57] Outside of them, bishops tended to relate not to one another but increasingly just with Rome.[58] The very ordering of the sections in *Lumen Gentium* invites us now to recognise a sacramental basis for episcopal collegiality in the Eucharist: because he is ordained to preside at the one Eucharist by which his own local church is bonded with all the others, each bishop is in solidarity with all his brothers in the episcopate. Since each is an icon of Christ the high priest among his people, all bishops, even in the furthest extremes of the earth, are united "in the mind of Christ," as Ignatius of Antioch taught,[59] and as Christ's care is for the church in its entirety, so must theirs be, in the deepest fraternal, or collegial, bond with one another.[60]

In a way, if the prayer for the ordination of a bishop from the *Apostolic Tradition* was reinstated after Vatican II, it would have been consistent to reinstate the ordination prayer for a presbyter

---

57. Kenan B. Osborne, *Priesthood: A History of Ordained Ministry in the Catholic Church* (Eugene, OR: Wipf and Stock, 2003), pp. 209–11.

58. Cf. Avery Dulles, "The Church as Communion," in Bradley Nassif, ed., *New Perspectives on Historical Theology* (Grand Rapids, MI: Eerdmans, 1996), pp. 125–39, here at p. 130: "reciprocity among equals was outweighed by jurisdiction from above." "The vertical lines of authority from Rome to the bishops replaced the horizontal lines of communion among bishops and among churches."

59. Cf. Ignatius of Antioch, *Ephesians* 3.

60. Cf. LG 22: "Together with their head, the Supreme Pontiff, and never apart from him, they [the bishops] have supreme and full authority over the universal Church."

also, but that of course was impossible. Major and long-standing developments made it inconceivable that those who were now priests should revert to being elders ordained to offer counsel to the bishop but not to preside at the liturgy.[61] Vatican II did reinstate the ancient title "presbyter" and used it much more frequently than English translations of the documents tend to indicate. It also restored the idea of the presbyterium gathered around the bishop in the life of the local church and in the liturgy, and cited Ignatius of Antioch as it did so.[62] Nevertheless, it firmly called such presbyters "true priests of the New Testament [*veri sacerdotes Novi Testamenti*],"[63] and a rather teasing question now arises in consequence: how are the priesthood of the bishop and that of the priest related? Is the bishop basically a priest like all the rest but with extra responsibility and authority, or is he the primary priest in his local church, upon whom the others depend in their priesthood? Pope John Paul seemed to align with the first view in his 1979 letter to priests, when he adapted the phrase of Augustine and said: *Vobis sum Episcopus, vobiscum sum Sacerdos* ("for you I am a bishop, with you I am a priest").[64] In light of Vatican II, however, which repeatedly teaches that in their ministry priests represent the bishop,[65] I wonder whether it might not be more appropriate for a bishop to say to his clergy: *with me you are priests.* In his celebration of the Eucharist, the presbyter is reliant on the communion that is manifested at the episcopal level in the church. That is why he names the bishop and indeed the pope in the eucharistic prayer that he says. The Eucharist intrinsically calls for visible bonds of communion.[66]

61. Moreover, as we have seen, there is at least a hint in the *Apostolic Tradition* that presbyters are priestly (see above, notes 32 and 33).

62. Cf. *Sacrosanctum Concilium* (SC) 41; LG 28; PO 7-8.

63. LG 28.

64. Pope John Paul II, Letter to Priests, *Novo incipiente nostro* (1979), 1.

65. Cf. SC 42; LG 28; PO 5.

66. Cf. Congregation for the Doctrine of the Faith, Letter to the Bishops of the Catholic Church on Some Aspects of the Church Understood as Communion, *Communionis Notio* (1992), n. 14: "The Unity of the Eucharist and the unity of the episcopate *with Peter and under Peter* are not independent roots of the unity of the Church, since Christ instituted the Eucharist and

Be that as it may, it seems to me that the restoration at the council of the idea that the bishop and his presbyterium form a team that cares for the local church was providential as the church began to face a clergy shortage and the difficulty of maintaining a priest in every parish. If parishes are viewed as communities within the local church as a whole, then the bishop with his body of presbyters, and of course increasingly a body of deacons also, has potentially a little more flexibility in his options as he seeks to make provision for his people.

One of the major advances in the council's teaching was its stress on the interaction that we saw earlier between the "ministerial or hierarchical priesthood," exercised in different degrees by the bishop and the presbyter, and the "common priesthood of the faithful." These priesthoods are quite distinct, but are "nonetheless ordered one to another; each in its own proper way shares [*participant*] in the one priesthood of Christ."[67] I would like to close by noting another major feature of the council's teaching with regard to Christ's priesthood and our participation in it. Completely absent from Vatican II was the scholastic scheme of power of order and power of jurisdiction, which heavily marked the difference between the ordained and the laity. In its place, the council developed the idea of the three offices (*munera*) of Christ, as prophet, priest, and king,[68] in which all members of the church, laity,[69] bishops,[70] presbyters,[71] and deacons,[72] all participate in their own proper ways, by virtue of their baptism or

---

the episcopate as essentially interlinked realities. The episcopate is *one*, just as the Eucharist is *one*: the one sacrifice of the one Christ, dead and risen" (emphasis in original).

67. LG 10.

68. Cf. LG 21, "teacher, shepherd and priest."

69. Cf. LG 31: "the faithful . . . in their own way share in the priestly, prophetic and kingly office [*munus*] of Christ"; also LG 34, 35.

70. Cf. LG 21.

71. Cf. LG 28: "they [presbyters] are consecrated in order to preach the Gospel and shepherd the faithful as well as to celebrate divine worship as true priests of the New Testament"; also, PO 1, 4-6.

72. Cf. LG 29: "they are dedicated to the People of God . . . in the service of the liturgy, of the Gospel and of works of charity."

ordination.[73] This threefold scheme, which has distant roots in the prayer for the offering of oil in the *Apostolic Tradition*, which recalls that kings, priests, and prophets were anointed by God in the Old Testament,[74] has a powerful unifying effect, emphasising that all members of the church, lay and ordained, are one in Christ and interrelated.

If the council tends to highlight Christ's *priesthood*, and to speak of a ministerial *priesthood* and a common *priesthood*, that is not to forget the other two offices of all concerned, but rather, I think, to suggest that priesthood acts to unify the three offices. Everything that Christ did, all of his teaching and service included, was done out of love for his Father and was taken up into the priestly offering of himself that he made to his Father on our behalf. Similarly, the council teaches that the faithful exercise their priesthood by "the reception of the sacraments, prayer and thanksgiving, the witness of a holy life, abnegation and active charity"[75]—everything they say and do is treated in this passage as material for their priestly offering; prophecy and service find their source and summit in priesthood. And the same is surely true of those ordained to the ministerial priesthood: all of our proclamation of the word and pastoral guidance flows into and out of what happens at the altar; we offer it in the sacrifice of Christ himself and pray that the Lord will make it fruitful. Again, priesthood embraces, integrates, and energises prophecy and

---

73. The teaching of LG 21 that episcopal consecration itself confers "the fulness of the sacrament of Orders," and "together with the office [*munus*] of sanctifying, the duty [*munera*] also of teaching and ruling," prompts the interesting question as to whether, though canon law stipulates it (cf. *Code of Canon Law*, can. 378) and pastoral prudence surely requires it, strictly speaking it is theologically necessary to be ordained as a presbyter before being ordained as a bishop. Within a scholastic understanding, of course, it was absolutely necessary to be ordained as a priest before being consecrated as a bishop. Cf. Susan K. Wood, *Sacramental Orders* (Collegeville, MN: Liturgical Press, 2000), pp. 166–71; James Monroe Barnett, *The Diaconate: A Full and Equal Order* (Harrisburg, PA: Trinity Press International, 1995), pp. 104–11.

74. *Apostolic Tradition*, §5, 2, in Bradshaw et al., *The Apostolic Tradition*, p. 50.

75. LG 10.

service. On the other hand, precisely so that we do not forget those essential accompanying activities of prophecy and service, it is good to call the priest a *presbyter*, which more readily evokes his broader responsibilities within the community.

Conclusion

In his encyclical letter, *Redemptor Hominis*, Pope John Paul said that "The Church wishes to serve this single end: that each person may be able to find Christ, in order that Christ may walk with each person the path of life."[76] To that end, it is the task of priests, in closest collaboration with the bishops, to nurture the life of Christ in the people of God and to form Christ in them, so that those who then encounter the faithful in all sorts of different contexts will find themselves also in the company of Christ. St. Paul wrote to the Galatians of his travail "until Christ is formed in you" (Gal 4:19), and it is worth recalling that in his letter to the Romans he referred to all of his apostolic ministry, all of his teaching, guidance, and travail, as "the priestly service of the gospel of God" (Rom 15:16). The council's remarkably rich Decree on the Ministry and Life of Priests—actually, of course, the term used was "presbyters" (*Decretum de Presbyterorum Ministerio et Vita*)—refers to this passage as it makes the following priestly point:

> Since they share in the function of the apostles in their own degree, presbyters are given the grace by God to be ministers of Jesus Christ among the nations, fulfilling the sacred task of the Gospel, that the oblation of the gentiles may be made acceptable and sanctified in the Holy Spirit. For it is by the apostolic herald of the Gospel that the People of God is called together and gathered so that all who belong to this people, sanctified as they are by the Holy Spirit, may offer themselves as "a living sacrifice, holy and acceptable to God" (Rom 12:1).[77]

---

76. Pope John Paul II, Encyclical Letter, *Redemptor Hominis* (1979), n. 13.
77. PO 2.

Those final words, too, come from Paul, as we saw earlier, which perhaps only serves to highlight how naturally the Year of St. Paul flows into the Year for Priests.

Chapter 5

A Spirituality for the Priest:
Apostolic, Relational, Liturgical

Monsignor Kevin W. Irwin

"Spirituality" is "hot copy" in America today. Books, tapes, CDs, DVDs, and internet sources about spirituality abound. As do sources about feeling close to God (or the divine), about feeling and being "religious," and about feeling and being "spiritual." There are also "self-help" guides for success, happiness, efficiency, and coping with life's highs and lows, one's addictions, and (fateful) attractions.

At the very same time within our church and across denominational lines the academic study of spirituality has come into its own as an important and rigorous discipline. (Among many others one need only note the contribution of Bernard McGinn in *The Essential Writings of Christian Mysticism*.[1]) We can say with pride that one of the features of the Catholic tradition is that we have many spiritual "families" and thus "spiritualities." Spirituality has also come into its own in the lives of parishioners and ministers. Necessary and important distinctions need to be made concerning the appropriate spiritual paths taken by the baptized layperson, the ordained (bishop, priest, and deacon), and those in consecrated life. Then there is the question of appropriate and necessary distinctions within the ranks of the ordained, e.g., diocesan, monastic, mendicant, religious, associations of diocesan

---

1. (New York: Random House, 2006.)

priests involved in a variety of ministries (e.g., priestly formation or the missions, foreign and home), etc. There are the appropriate and necessary distinctions within religious communities and congregations spanning the gamut from those in monasteries with fixed times and patterns of daily liturgical (and other) prayer to those whose apostolates in church institutions and in the marketplace can (at least seem to) be 24/7. One size does not fit all when it comes to Christian spirituality. That is because one size does not fit all when it comes to living the Christian vocation. Nor does one size fit all when leading the priestly life.

My reflections in this presentation are intended for priests engaged in the apostolic ministry,[2] by which I mean in the day-to-day apostolate of church work and church life. These include, among others, ministry in the parish, teaching, formation, administration, campus, and other kinds of "hands on" ministry. Obviously these ministries place priests in direct relationship with the people of God. These ministries serve as the direct experience of pastoral ministry that I want to presume and that is the context for framing what I shall call *an apostolic, relational, liturgical spirituality*. My presumption throughout will be about immediate and direct encounter with the people priests uniquely serve in liturgy and in sacraments as well as in the range of tasks and ministries that priests normally engage in.

What I want to argue in this presentation is that the celebration of the liturgy is intrinsic to the way that all Catholics live their vocations, and that the liturgy is at the heart of the prayer, spirituality, and the spiritual life of all Catholic Christians. It is also intrinsic to the life of the priest. The question that underlies this presentation is *what role should the liturgy play in an apostolic, relational spirituality that is suited for priests?* Allow me to take two of the operative words here and explain how I understand them in what follows—*liturgy* and *spirituality*.

---

2. There is a wide use of the term "apostolic," which in some monastic literature means that the monks live in imitation of the first apostles, especially as gathered together, exemplified in the summaries in the Acts of the Apostles 2:42 about the idealized early Christian communities.

Liturgy

In the year 2000 I was asked by the editors of *Church* magazine to address the phenomenon of what was then called "the liturgy wars." In that article I argued that it was important to distinguish between liturgical *reforms* (tasks to do, books to publish, churches to (re)build, ministers to train, presiding skills to hone) and liturgical *renewal*, which is hopefully served by the liturgy's reforms but which are the means to the goal—which goal is nothing less than the continual communal conversion to the Gospel and to the enlivening of the church through the liturgy.[3]

I mention this (for me important) distinction because I want to voice my concern that for some of late the externals of the liturgy have become something of a curiosity. There seems to be an increasing concern for rubrics, clothing, direction of the priest and people at Mass, the way priests choose to preside or when the manner of priests' presiding becomes an object of curiosity, not to say dissent. If these externals become *the* focus or how we understand the liturgy, then we have lost the meaning of what liturgy does and is. In what follows I want to go beyond "the liturgy wars" and emphasizing externals to the inner meaning and dynamic of the liturgy. Liturgy's externals are important. But they are means, not ends.

Liturgy is the celebration of the paschal mystery of Christ in communities of faith presided over by the ordained in ritual actions through words, gestures, signs, and symbols that are a privileged means to the end, which is nothing less than communal and personal self-transcendence and conversion to the Gospel, as we await and welcome the coming of God's kingdom in its fullness.

Among the questions I continually ask myself are:

- Priests are ordained to serve the people of God. How is their relationship with the people they serve factored into the spiritual life of the priest?

- Do not the changes in church structures after Vatican II (e.g., parish councils, presbyteral councils, other collaborative

---

3. "Getting Beyond the Liturgy Wars," *Church* (Fall 2000). Winner Second Place, Best Article of 2000, Catholic Press Association Award.

bodies, advisory boards, and all sorts of meetings with parishioners) need to be taken into account in laying out the shape of a priest's spirituality today in terms of collaboration and collegiality?

- Does not the revision of the liturgy after Vatican II offer a new context in terms of public liturgical ministry that should be a mainstay of priestly spirituality?

- If "more is required" for the celebration of the post–Vatican II liturgy "than the mere observance of the laws governing valid and lawful celebration" (*Liturgy Constitution* 11)[4] then would not a deeper exploration of the theology of the liturgy and of what the liturgy does in its uniqueness be important mainstays for the spirituality of a priest?

You will not be surprised that given my own theological expertise and close to forty-something years experience as a parish priest in academe that my thesis is that *the liturgy articulates and shapes the range of relationships in which the (parish) priest is involved and that the celebration of the liturgy gives shape and right order to those relationships. These are (regularly) articulated in the prayers and rites of the liturgy priests are privileged to preside over.*

Spirituality

Definitions and descriptions of *spirituality* abound. If you Google the word "spirituality" in .08 seconds you will get 47,400,000 suggested sites. Allow me to dare to enter this fray by offering the working definition of "spirituality" that I should like to use as part of framing my discussion of an appropriate spirituality for the priest.

Let me offer a working definition. *Spirituality is a way of thinking and acting shaped primarily by the church's corporate experience of God, who is immanent and transcendent, revealed yet remains hidden, a triune God who invites us into deep and abiding relationship with*

---

4. The rest of the text reads: "It is [the duty of pastors] to ensure that the faithful take part fully aware of what they are doling, actively engaged in the rite, and enriched by its effects" (DOL trans., p. 7).

Father, Son, and Holy Spirit and through them to the whole church and the wider world. Spirituality enables church members to maintain corporate values and minority positions with confidence in the face of contrary cultural pressures because of the power of God's enlivening Spirit within and among us. Spirituality guides a person's understanding of the world and it provides a basis for discipline in one's life.

While it is obvious, allow me simply to note that what underlies this definition is a Catholic worldview and a Catholic way of looking at and reflecting on the spiritual life. Simply put, "spirituality" is more than one's prayer, or participation in the liturgy, or one's devotional practices. It is in fact a worldview that determines how we look at life and live the life of God.

A crucial factor in articulating an *apostolic, relational, liturgical spirituality* is to understand that what makes liturgy so important is that it is the church's privileged *experience* of and *participation* in the very being of God, with and among the community gathered by God to share in the very life of God in order that we might live the life of God in the world. Liturgy does not describe or define these relationships. Liturgy is the privileged and unique forum in which these relationships are set in proper order and are experienced.

Allow me to name the relationships I see as intrinsic to the life and ministry of the priest as they undergird what I am calling an apostolic, relational spirituality. As I note them I want to refer to the way the liturgy names and presumes them. In effect I want to emphasize how these relationships are understood and experienced in and through the celebration of the liturgy. Among those relationships are the following—they are very familiar to the priest engaged in the apostolic ministry!

God

The first and underlying relationship is with God, Father, Son, and Spirit. The Judeo-Christian God of the Scriptures and the God of our Catholic tradition is a God who invites us as a people into a relationship that is deep, abiding, sustaining, and nurturing. One of the Sunday prefaces (VI) refers to St. Paul's speech on the Areopagus, which captures the relational character of the God we believe in and live in: "in him we live and move and have our being" (Acts 17:28). It is followed by the phrase:

> Each day you show us a Father's love;
> your Holy Spirit, dwelling within us,
> gives us on earth the hope of unending joy.[5]

Even as we acknowledge God's utter transcendence, texts such as this remind us that we believe and abide in a relational God. This is a dynamic, biblical, and liturgical way of expressing the conventional Catholic assertion that we are "temples of the Holy Spirit."

After this primary and foundational relationship with God the following other relationships are to be seen in relation to each other and to God as their absolute foundation. In effect they might be imaged as circles within the widest circle who is God and our relatedness to God in the church.

Church Leaders, Church Universal and Local

One who is ordained is privileged to give voice at the liturgy, specifically in the eucharistic prayer, to our relatedness to and prayer with and for church leaders. The naming of the pope and bishop in every eucharistic prayer is a statement of Catholic ecclesiology. No individual act of liturgy is ever "just" of this community gathered here and now. It is always of the wider diocesan and world church even as it is an act of this particular gathered assembly. Priests are ordained by the bishop for the service of the church, even as a variety of priests are ordained for and with their particular religious communities, institutes, societies, and dioceses. The naming of the pope and local bishop serves as a continual reminder of the wider church lens that is always a part of Catholicism. It is also an invitation to continue to pray for and with them in their essential ministries for the church. From a

---

5. *Sacramentary for Mass* (New York: Catholic Book Publishing Co., 1985) 439.

slightly different point of view this helps prevent any given liturgy and context for liturgy from being too focused on itself or oneself. This is often termed "congregationalism" and is not a natively Catholic way of looking at church belonging or liturgical participation.

Priest—Presbyters

Priests are ordained into the "order of presbyters." They are not ordained in isolation or as individuals. One of the key elements of the theology of orders that is expressed in the documents of Vatican II and is in the title of the revised ordination rites is that all ordinations are to the "order of bishops," to the "order of presbyters," to the "order of deacons." The clear shift in the language of Vatican II to describe what we have come to call "priestly" ordination as ordination to the *presbyterate* is a major theological statement that needs to be reflected on and underscored as we describe the "the priestly life" and "priestly spirituality."[6] Again this points to the relational character of one's priestly ordination. The priest is ordained into a preexisting body of fellow presbyter-priests. For many priests this is their "first line" of support and challenge. Some priests live in stable religious houses and thus experience presbyteral relatedness on a day-to-day basis. Among other implications of this collegial understanding of the presbyterate is the opportunity to view the priestly character as less something that one receives for oneself but rather something that binds us together with other presbyters. Such an approach reflective of the Vatican II emphasis on ecclesiology and collegiality would be a development from what has legitimately been argued to be a comparatively individualist understanding of the priestly character expressed at the Council of Trent.[7]

---

6. Among others see the excellent study by Paul Josef Cordes, *Sendung zum Dienst*, Exegetische-historische und systematische Studien zum Konsilsdekret, "Vom Dienst und Leben der Priester" (Frankfurt am Main: Josef Knecht, 1972).

7. Among others see, Ganoczy, Alexander, "Splendors and Miseries of the Tridentine Doctrine of Ministries," *Office and Ministry in the Church*, Concilium

Other Pastoral Ministers

The phenomenon of lay ecclesial ministers in today's American church (whose formation and education is carefully articulated in *Coworkers in the Vineyard*[8]) is a fact of vibrant American Catholic pastoral life. These include (with varying titles and job descriptions) (permanent) deacon, pastoral associate, faith formation director, school principal and teachers, liturgical ministry director, youth ministers, social justice coordinators, etc. Priests know and rely on this. These are truly the priest's "coworkers." Regular meetings during which pastoral staffs share information and projects and at which they debate future plans in their ministries are staples of parish life today. Priests know only too well that the names listed on the front cover of the parish bulletin and the homepage of the parish's website are the people without whom the parish could not function. It is often said that the vitality of the life of the Catholic Church in America is due to the myriad ministries and high level of functioning of the parish. This presumes a high degree of cooperation among those on the parish staff—all of whom are related to each other and to the priest.

Staff

While parishes are not businesses there are numberless ways in which parish staff personnel carry out the "business" functions of a parish: secretaries, receptionists, accountants, maintenance, etc. The parish priest is aware of and legitimately presumes on their cooperation, work, and support. In turn part of his responsibility is to relate to them in a collaborative and respectful way.

Lay Volunteers

Parishes presume on the personal gifts and most often freely given talents of a variety of parishioners. The range is enormous, from RCIA team members to liturgical ministers, choir members,

80, ed. Roland Murphy and Bas van Iersel (New York: Herder and Herder, 1972) pp. 75–86, and Hervé-Marie Legrand, "The Indelible Character and the Theology of Ministry," pp. 54–62.
  8. See www.usccb.org/laity/laymin/co-workers.

extraordinary ministers of Communion to the sick and home-bound, catechists, food pantry and soup kitchen volunteers, etc. Lay "involvement" is almost a redundant term. It is the range of lay volunteers who help the parish to function and to have the variety of ministries it is engaged in. This is "people-to-people" ministry. Like all of us, priests have certain gifts and talents. But we do not possess all the gifts and talents on which the folks rely. It takes the full complement of laypeople to make it "work."

Parishioners and Those We Serve

The ongoing day-to-day ministry of the priest is predicated on his relationship with "the folks"—parishioners, students, etc. As obvious as it sounds, priests are there to serve the liturgical and myriad other needs of the people of Christ. Appropriate pastoral care reflects the priest's knowledge of those he serves and vice versa.

That the demands of the apostolate are at the heart of a priest's life is reflected in this text from the Office of Readings on the feast of St. Vincent de Paul (Sept. 27):

> Do not become upset or feel guilty because you interrupted your prayer to serve the poor. God is not neglected if you leave him for such service. One of God's works is merely interrupted so that another can be carried out. So when you leave prayer to serve some poor person, remember that this very service is performed for God. Charity is certainly greater than any rule. Moreover all rules must lead to charity.[9]

What is the life of the priest all about but living the life of God with and among the sets of relationships God sets before us? Spirituality is not "getting away from it all"; it is putting those relationships into proper order and growing in holiness in the midst of those relationships. Who does that? God. One central way that God does that for us again and again is in and through

---

9. *The Liturgy of the Hours,* Volume Four (New York: Catholic Book Publishing Co., 1975), p. 1425.

the liturgy. Our privilege and responsibility is to preside at and preach at the sacred liturgy—for our sakes and the sanctification of the whole church.

To be realistic and workable a priest's spirituality must take account of and be very aware of these (and other) sets of relationships in which he is involved. An appropriate *apostolic, relational, liturgical spirituality* is one where all of these relationships are all manifest and where they are reshaped, reformed, and renewed. I will argue from experience what you yourselves regularly experience and know well: there is a world of difference between celebrating the liturgy in a community to which you are a part and whom you regularly serve and covering a Mass on a substitute basis. It is in the regular celebration of the liturgy with and for the same community of faith that the relationships I have articulated are forged, deepened, and made richer. Priests know that instinctively when we meet and greet the folks on their way into and out of church, when we pray with and for them in the prayer of the faithful, and when we distribute Communion, we are part of their lives and their lives are part of our lives. The hands and faces we see at Communion are the kaleidoscope of images and likenesses that comprise the church in miniature at every celebration of the Eucharist.

In addition to fostering these (and other) relationships, priests know well that the real life of the priest involves a myriad of tasks for their dioceses and religious communities, such as service on committees and councils as well as following diocesan or provincial policies and procedures; it involves a myriad of tasks that include administration, education, supervision, spiritual direction, counseling, etc. (As a sometime "manager" of university personnel I am thinking here of the phrase in personnel manuals and contracts: "and other duties as assigned!"). The real life of the priest in parish ministry is unpredictable, especially when it is compared with other full-time ministries such as education and diocesan administration. Priests in parishes often say to me that my evenings are relatively "free" and their evenings are relatively "unfree." Meetings (especially evening meetings) are material for contemporary asceticism—for numberless reasons that priests can describe without preparation!

I want to argue that these sets of relationships and these tasks (and likely many others) all need to be factored into a spirituality for the priest simply because he is involved in all of them (and indeed more). There should be a "relational consciousness" to a priest's spirituality simply because of his immersion in these sets of relationships, all of which are articulated and expressed in and through the priest's "pastoral liturgical ministry." All liturgy is pastoral in that it is celebrated for and with the people of God. Liturgy is always about God and the mediation of God's life to the communities of faith that the priest is privileged to serve— both in liturgy and in the variety of tasks that together comprise the priest's "job description."

In light of this I should like to argue that a major part of the priest's growth in holiness—his *sanctification*—occurs in and through the celebration of the liturgy among God's holy people. I have often asked my students to review the texts of the liturgy and to see that almost all of the terms that refer to human beings are in the plural. This intersects with the fact that the liturgy is the celebration of "the work of our redemption" (prayer over the gifts, Evening Mass of the Lord's Supper) in the assembled community. It is always the enactment of the mystery of faith for and with each other. The pronouns in the prayers of the church's liturgy almost always articulate relatedness: "*we* pray through Christ our Lord," "*we* offer you this sacrifice of praise for ourselves and those who are dear to us," "Lord hear *our* prayer." Those are the normal pronouns the priest himself articulates when he celebrates the liturgy for and with the people. The fundamental ecclesial consciousness evident here should lead to an appreciation that the priest prays *in the person of Christ* and also *in the person of the church*—to use a theological shorthand.[10]

Priestly Life and Job Satisfaction

Almost immediately after Vatican II the American bishops commissioned a series of studies about "the American priest-

---

10. The phrase *in persona Christi capitis ecclesiae* and variations on it are consistently used in the document of Vatican II and in Pope John Paul II's Holy Thursday Letters to Priests.

hood." These included sociological studies undertaken in 1970, 1985, and 1993 about what might well be called "job satisfaction."[11]

In addition two (comparatively brief) documents published by the bishops' conference at the same time that were very influential on many American priests in the immediate post–Vatican II years were the *Spiritual Renewal of the American Priesthood* and *As One Who Serves*, aimed at supporting priests as they developed their spiritual lives in light of the of the documents of Vatican II and the changes that occurred in American parish life as consequences of the council's decrees. These bishops' conference documents are particularly notable because they were among the first to speak about the influence that the reformed liturgy can and should have on the spiritual lives of priests. These were published in the immediate aftermath of Vatican II and were intended to help priests to appreciate the reformed liturgy as a central means of shaping their ministerial and spiritual lives. They also noted that presiding and preaching at the vernacular liturgy offered great stimulus to the spiritual growth of priests.

We priests know well that we are ordained, we are not simply commissioned or deputed. There are important theological realities implied by the word "ordination." One of the meanings of the Latin term *ordinatio* is "to set [or be set] in proper order." What is presiding and preaching but the way to put all of our lives in proper order? In a sense our ordination is for the sake of our people and ourselves to be set in proper order. And what more privileged means for this is there than the celebration of the liturgy for and with the people we serve?

Priestly Sanctification

One of Pope Benedict XVI's concerns in establishing the "Year for Priests" is "to deepen the commitment of all priests to interior

---

11. See the helpful summary in Dean R. Hoge, Joseph J. Shields, and Douglas L. Griffin, "Changes in Satisfaction and Institutional Attitudes of Catholic Priests, 1970–1993," *Sociology of Religion* 56:2 (1995) as well as *Evolving Visions of the Priesthood*, Changes from Vatican II to the Turn of the New Century (Collegeville: Liturgical Press, 2003); and Dean Hoge, *The First Five Years of the Priesthood* (Collegeville: Liturgical Press, 2002).

renewal for the sake of a more forceful and incisive witness to the Gospel in today's world."[12] In a number of places he refers to the priest's sanctification. In doing so he underscores a perennial challenge and opportunity for the priest—how to grow in holiness in the midst of all of his ministerial responsibilities? My argument would be that the liturgy is *the* catalyst, *the* source, *the* means for priest's sanctification to occur.

As far back as Pope Pius X in 1903 church documents have asserted that the sacred liturgy is aimed toward "the glory of God and the sanctification and edification of the people."[13] The Constitution on the Sacred Liturgy of Vatican II reiterates this in four places: when it refers to the use of signs in the liturgy (n. 7), about how all other activities of the church are directed to the Eucharist because it is especially here that humans' sanctification is accomplished (n. 10), that both sacramentals and sacraments sanctify almost every event in human life (n. 61), and (repeating Pius X's assertion above) that "the purpose of sacred music . . . is the glory of God and the sanctification of the faithful" (n. 112). Pope John Paul II enhanced this highly christological emphasis to include the Holy Spirit in his encyclical on the *Eucharist in the Life of the Church* (n. 17) when he cited the important theological point about the epiclesis part of the eucharistic prayer: "God the Father is asked to send the Holy Spirit upon the faithful and upon the offerings, so that the body and blood of Christ 'may be a help to all those who partake of it . . . for the sanctification of their souls and bodies.' The Church is fortified by the divine Paraclete through the sanctification of the faithful in the Eucharist" (n. 23).[14]

The designation of the consecrated bread and wine as "holy things for the holy people of God" as found in some eastern

---

12. Pope Benedict XVI, Letter "Proclaiming a Year for Priests," June 16, 2009, para. 1, www.vatican.va/.../benedict_xvi/homilies/.../hf_ben-xvi _hom_20090619_anno-sac_en.html.

13. Pope Pius X, *Tra le Sollecitudini*, Instruction on Sacred Music, Nov. 22, 1903, n. 1.

14. www.vatican.va/.../hf_jp-ii_enc_20030417_ecclesia_eucharistia _en.html

liturgical sources and as reiterated in the *Catechism of the Catholic Church*[15] reflects how the food of the Eucharist exemplifies how the liturgy is celebrated for our spiritual nourishment—for our interior renewal and for our communal and individual sanctification. If this is clearly true for the whole people of God who celebrate the liturgy it is particularly true of the priest who presides over the liturgy.

In fact I want to argue that it is precisely in the act of presiding at the liturgy that the priest's sanctification occurs in as rich a way as is possible. If liturgy is our *participation*—our *"taking part in"* Christ's paschal mystery—and this is the act by which we have been redeemed, it stands to reason that this is indeed the ritual enactment and our communal experience of the paschal mystery as the "mystery of faith" should be the "summit and source" or our sanctification. The priest who presides has a unique and privileged role to play in this enactment of our salvation and the accomplishment of our (continual) sanctification. For some this kind of approach may offer a challenge to move from understanding our vocations as "dispensing grace" to an engagement in the grace that God dispenses through the liturgy at which we preside. This approach to a liturgical spirituality is less about what we do, and far more about what God does for us in the liturgy. At the same time this understanding of priestly spirituality centered in the liturgy means that we need to be attentive to and careful about what it means to preside and preach at the liturgy.

We priests grow in holiness in the midst of the relationships that our various apostolates place before us. We priests grow in holiness by presiding and preaching at the various liturgies that our ministries demand of us. We priests grow in holiness not in order to face our pastoral responsibilities but by engaging in our

---

15. *Catechism of the Catholic Church*, 1331. "[The Eucharist is called] Holy Communion, because by this sacrament we unite ourselves to Christ, who makes us sharers in his Body and Blood to form a single body. We also call it: the holy things (*ta hagia*; sancta)—the first meaning of the phrase 'communion of saints' in the Apostles' Creed—the bread of angels, bread from heaven, medicine of immortality, viaticum."

pastoral responsibilities that include direct pastoral care, presiding, and preaching.

Presiding at Liturgy

But in reality the act of presiding and preaching at liturgy is work, a work undertaken long before the celebration begins. Part and parcel of every act of liturgy is knowing the folks and coming to know them at ever deeper and richer levels. We priests know that there is no such thing as a repeated liturgy. We may use the same books and texts, proclaim the same readings and prayers of the liturgy, and even the same music at the liturgy. But each and every celebration of the liturgy is different because it is a different community of faith, or changed world situations, church contexts, changes in the personal lives of those gathered there, both personally and communally.

To preside at liturgy is not simply to engage in "a ceremony." It is always the articulation and experience of the church's highs and lows, successes and failures, spiritual triumphs and spiritual dryness. It is always with and always for the people of God.

We do not "just" preside at a baptism. We are part of the lives of those who present themselves for baptism or full communion because of the RCIA structures and rituals (not to say work!). We are part of the lives of those who present their children for baptism. Priests know the prayer for blessing water (almost) by heart. When they pray these words it is within the assembly of believers. It is with their lives and needs uppermost in his mind:

> Father,
> Look now with love upon your Church
> And unseal for it the fountain of baptism.
> By the power of the Holy Spirit
> Give to this water the grace of your Son,
> So that in the sacrament of baptism
> All those whom you have created in your likeness
> May be cleansed from sin
> And rise to a new birth of innocence
> By water and the Holy Spirit.
> (celebrant touches water)

We ask you, Father, with your Son
To send the Holy Spirit upon the waters of this font.
May all who are buried with Christ in the death of baptism
Rise also with him to newness of life.

We do not "just" hear confessions. We share in the experience of grace shared with those who come to unburden themselves to us and through us to experience the untying of bonds that oppress and relieve burdens that weigh down. In the sacrament of penance we engage in appropriate direction and spiritual counsel and offer the healing words of absolution to take away their sins as they and we move ahead and forward in the spiritual life.

Through the ministry of the church
May God give you pardon and peace
And I absolve you in the name of the Father . . .

We do not "just" anoint the sick. Rather we engage in a humbling experience of welcoming the obviously ill into the embrace of the church's celebration of this sacrament (or in an emergency when we as the priest arrive on the scene) to impose hands and anoint with oil those foreheads whose brows are often tightly knit in tension, anger, frustration, bewilderment, and pain. We anoint hands that may well be crippled, discolored, or dry with too many antiseptic washings and cleansings, with arms that have been pricked and punctured all too many times with injections to draw blood to check for medical progress or injections with medicine to mitigate pain and suffering. We pray:

"Through this holy anointing, may the Lord in his love and mercy help you with the grace of the Holy Spirit."

"May the Lord who frees you from sin save you and raise you up."

We do not "just" preside at a Sunday Mass. Rather we have the privilege of celebrating with the gathered assembly of the people of Christ week in and week out whose struggles in the faith may well be known to us alone so that when we pray "strengthen in faith and love your pilgrim church on earth" (third Eucharistic Prayer) we call to mind and heart those in that congregation who have doubts of faith as did Thomas the Apostle, who may have denied knowing Christ as did St. Peter, who may have sinned exceedingly in the flesh as did David and Bathsheba in the OT and as imaged in countless depictions of Mary of Magdala. We also pray that they and we might be immersed in the paschal mystery of Christ as members of each other in the ever more unified pilgrim church on earth.

> (from the Roman Canon)
>
> Father, we celebrate the memory of Christ, your Son.
> we your people and your ministers
> recall his passion, his resurrection from the dead,
> and his ascension into glory;
> and from the many gifts you have given us
> we offer to you, God of glory and majesty,
> this holy and perfect sacrifice. . . .
>
> Then, as we receive from this altar the sacred body and blood
>   of your Son,
> Let us be filled with every grace and blessing.
>
> (from Eucharistic Prayer III)
>
> Father, calling to mind the death your Son endured for our
>   salvation,
> His glorious resurrection and ascension into heaven,
> And ready to greet him when he comes again, we offer you in
>   thanksgiving this holy and living sacrifice.
> Grant that we, who are nourished by his body and blood,
> May be filled with his Holy Spirit and become one body, one
>   spirit in Christ.

Every priest knows these texts only too well. Their theology reflects the essentially ecclesial nature of what the liturgy is and his role in it.

Liturgy for and with the People

Instinctively priests know that the liturgy is celebrated by, with, and for the folks in direct relation to their need for pastoral care.

Pastoral care is the presumed context for liturgy and liturgy should always reflect pastoral care. This is what gives liturgy its lived context. It is what gives the celebration of the liturgy its vitality. *Liturgy derives from and returns us to the day-to-day life context of those who celebrate it.*

Day-to-day ministering with others and day-to-day pastoral care shapes the life of the priest in numberless ways. This is an incarnational spirituality whereby we regularly experience Christ's presence among us in our daily, ministerial lives. Experiencing Christ in the people to whom he ministers offers the priest a privileged, sacred trust. And it is these relationships with parishioners in whatever need that forms the context for what is celebrated in and through the liturgy. These sets of ministerial relationships shape the daily prayer of the priest. His personal prayer at the intercessions at the Hours and at the Eucharist cannot help but be directly shaped by these ministerial experiences. In fact, I would argue, it is these day-to-day pastoral experiences that give life and vitality to the priest's personal and liturgical life. They cannot but help to influence him as he prepares the Sunday homily, especially as he faces those people and leads them in the Eucharist on Sunday. Therefore there is a presumed *integration* between liturgy and pastoral care. And it is this presumed integration that makes the liturgy always a vital and new experience for the priest.

Challenges

Allow me to offer four challenges to what I have offered here as one way of approaching a contemporary priestly spirituality.

Communal Spirituality

One of the challenges for understanding and embracing *spirituality* is that it is about nothing less than the spiritual *life*, here understood to be the priestly *life*. Spirituality is about our lives lived with and among others as we, corporately and individually, abide in and experience the presence and action of the living God. Ultimately a characteristic feature of a Catholic spirituality is that it is communally and personally self-transcending. More specifically, Catholic spirituality is not about oneself (alone). But we do live in a culture that prizes oneself. And we live in a society that from the beginning did emphasize the rights and duties of individuals. While there is much good that can and needs to be derived from the self-help books and materials alluded to earlier, I wonder whether the emphasis on the self is too preoccupying (not to say assumed?) when one thinks about spirituality. What good is "self-help" if the only one who gets helped is the self? That is not Catholic spirituality or Catholic life. Spirituality is about ourselves in relation to others and how we live with and among each other. There is a danger that some of what passes for "spirituality" today (e.g., feeling "spiritual" or "religious") is concerned with the self only. Then it is narcissism. In Catholicism we always go to God together. Catholicism is an ecclesiological tradition. In Catholicism the spiritual life is always lived in community, corporately and in *communio*.

Fellow Presbyters

I would like to offer three thoughts under this category that I judge to be a "work in progress" on many levels, among which are:

Theologically. It is very clear that the fathers at the Second Vatican Council wanted to revive the term *presbyter* when referring to what we have customarily called *priests*. This term is found in the New Testament and patristic era to delineate those in the "college of presbyters" and coworkers with the bishop but not in the episcopal order. The term *priest* came to replace "presbyter" as the emphasis in eucharistic theology and ministry was on the power of the priest (presbyter or bishop) to consecrate the Eucharist. The restoration of the term "presbyter" was an important theological statement at Vatican. However, since then more often than not the term "priest" is omnipresent in describing the "order of presbyters." Even the Vatican II document *Presbyterorum Ordinis* is most often translated as the "Decree on the Life and Ministry of Priests." I judge that the understanding of "priest" over "presbyter" can be too limiting. In fact "presbyter language" is envisioned in the life and ministry of those ordained as the bishops' coworkers.

Structurally. While theologically in the church's documents of Vatican II and since and liturgically in the revised rites of ordination after Vatican II the relationship of the college of presbyters and the diocesan bishop is clearly underscored I think that in practice this relationship and relatedness is difficult to achieve. Simply put, diocesan priests are assigned with few others, or anyone else, and are called to minister in the bishop's name but not in any real proximity to a college of presbyters. Some dioceses have annual or semi-annual clergy days and convocations that go a long way toward securing this kind of collegial relationship. The same is true for presbyteral councils. But an intimate knowledge of the priests by the bishop (they are called "his" priests in *Lumen Gentium* 28) is not always achievable, especially in large archdioceses or in rural dioceses.

Personally. On a more personal level I also want to offer the challenge that our priestly fraternity is often marred by offhand comments that put each other down. I wonder why it is that jealousy often leads to inappropriate rhetoric rather than rhetoric that builds up and supports the presbyterate. I think we need to admit that sometimes our words about priests are nothing less than acts of verbal fratricide. We are ordained into the college of presbyters because we are in this together.

Diminished Ability to Know the Folks

Priests know well that their ability to get to know (well) a stable community of the faithful is not always easy given the reduction in the number of the ordained and the demands placed on them. The "consolidation" of parishes has often meant that priests serve in more than one parish and celebrate sacraments in more than one location. The overly facile term "the weekend warrior," to describe the priest who serves sparingly during the week and is omnipresent on Sunday, can now be used to describe how many priests have to move from parish to parish on a weekend to take care of the needs of the faithful to participate in Sunday Mass. (This is not to mention the phenomenon when priests are unable to be present, especially for long periods of time, when *Sunday Worship in the Absence of a Priest* is used.) This makes it all the more difficult for the priest to get to know the parishioners in ways that were customary a generation ago. For those priests in stable communities this is a challenge but any and every attempt to engage and be engaged with the folks outside of the liturgy can go a long way toward supporting the kind of spirituality based on the liturgy that is presumed here. I must confess that I fear that without efforts to support the priest's coming to know the people well we are at the risk of ever increasing "anonymous" celebrations of the Eucharist and of liturgy in general.

Ministries not Ministers

One of the most important aspects of post–Vatican II church life in the United States has been the revitalization of the variety of ministries that have flourished in our church. But I sometimes wonder whether the emphasis placed on *ministry* is all too often accompanied by a presumption that it is about the *ministers* themselves. In theory we know well that it is always a matter of balancing my gifts and talents with those of the entire church, especially at the liturgy. I have already argued that liturgical ministry is not anonymous. But it should not be attention grabbing or "in your face" either. Both USCCB documents *Music in Catholic Worship* and *Sing to the Lord* contain the assertion that "no single factor affects the celebration as the manner of the priest celebrant."[16] To my mind this is a helpful encouragement about the kind of ministry in which we are engaged and that the way we do it matters very much. But I also wonder whether this might be a way of underscoring the post-Tridentine model of liturgy when it is the priest's role that is all important. All ministries and ministers are important—including the engagement of the gathered assembly in the worship of God. And again the way each of us ministers is important. There is a world of difference, I would argue, between "speak Lord, I love to listen to your voice" and a performance (literally!) of that psalm that really says "speak Lord, I love to listen to *my* voice!"

---

16. www.usccb.org/liturgy/SingToTheLord.pdf, n. 18.

I often say that I have one role model and one patron saint from the gospels for myself and, I should think, for the priest. My role model is from the parable of the sower sowing seeds of the Word of God (Mark 4:1-9 and par.). All I try to do is to sow the seeds as faithfully and fully as I can. I cannot predict the good soil. I cannot plan how the Word of God is heard and appropriated. But I do know that it is my responsibility to try as best I can to preach that Word faithful and fully.

My patron saint is John the Baptist. He gave voice to what we priests know only too well. "He must increase. I must decrease."

Conclusion

In this presentation I have argued the importance of experiencing the liturgy as the center of a priest's apostolic, relational spirituality. But this presumes an understanding of the liturgy that it is first and foremost about what God has done and does for us in Christ by the power of the Holy Spirit. It is not done under our own power. As the influential Benedictine liturgist Aidan Kavanagh once said, "we do liturgy" but fundamentally "liturgy does us." Liturgy is our continual and ever deepening incorporation into the paschal dying and rising of Christ in the community of the gathered church. Its texts and rites are a given for us to appropriate and through them to be assimilated into God.

We priests are privileged to preside and preach at the liturgy. We have a crucial and central role. But there are several other roles and ministries in which a variety of coworkers and faithful Christians are engaged. We need to take our ministries very seriously. But as Cardinal Basil Hume once said to the novice monks at Ampleforth Abbey, "Take God very seriously, take your vocation seriously, but do not take yourselves too seriously!"

I also have said more than once that I think that were I to wade into the waters of bumper sticker design I would manufacture one for all the priests that I know. It would simply be "Jn. 1:20," which is the response of John the Baptist to his questioners about who he is. In many translations John asserts "I am not the Messiah."

Appendix: Comparison of Ordination Prayers, 1975 and 2003

ORDINATION OF A PRIEST (ET 1975)

Prayer of Consecration

Come to our help,
Lord, holy Father, almighty and eternal God;
you are the source of every honor and dignity,
of all progress and stability.
You watch over the growing family of man
by your gift of wisdom and your pattern of order.

When you had appointed high priests to rule your people,
you chose other men next to them in rank and dignity
to be with them and to help them in their task;
and so there grew up
[the ranks of priests and the offices of levites,]
established by sacred rites.

In the desert
you extended the spirit of Moses to seventy wise men
who helped him to rule the great company of his people.

You shared among the sons of Aaron
the fullness of their father's power,
to provide worthy priests in sufficient number
[for the increasing rites of sacrifice and worship.]

ORDINATION OF PRIESTS (ET 2003)

Prayer of Ordination

Draw near, O Lord, holy Father,
almighty and eternal God,
author of **human dignity**:
it is you who apportion all **graces**,
through you everything progresses;
through you all things are made to stand firm.
To form a priestly people
you appoint ministers of Christ your Son
by the power of the Holy Spirit,
arranging them in different orders.

Already in the earlier covenant
offices arose, established through mystical rites:
when you set Moses and Aaron over your people
to govern and sanctify them,
you chose men next in rank and dignity
to accompany them and assist them in their task.

So too in the desert you implanted the spirit of Moses
in the hearts of seventy wise men;
and with their help he ruled your people with greater ease.

So also upon the sons of Aaron
you poured an abundant share of their father's plenty,
that the number of the priests prescribed by the Law
might be sufficient for the **sacrifices of the tabernacle,**
which were a shadow of the good things to come.

ORDINATION OF A PRIEST (ET 1975), *continued*

[With the same loving care
 you gave companions to your Son's apostles
to help in teaching the faith:
they preached the Gospel to the whole world.]

[Lord,
grant also to us such fellow workers,
for we are weak and our need is greater.]

Almighty Father,
grant to this servant of yours
the dignity of the priesthood.
Renew within him the Spirit of holiness.
As a co-worker with the order of bishops
may he be faithful to the ministry
that he receives from you, Lord God,
and be to others a model of right conduct.

May he be faithful in working with the order of bishops,
so that the words of the Gospel may reach the ends of the earth,

ORDINATION OF PRIESTS (ET 2003), *continued*

But in these last days, holy Father,
you sent your Son into the world,
Jesus, who is Apostle and High Priest of our confession.
Through the Holy Spirit
he offered himself to you as a spotless victim;
and he made his Apostles, consecrated in the truth,
sharers in his mission.
You provided them also with companions
to proclaim and carry out the work of salvation
throughout the whole world.
And now we beseech you, Lord, in our weakness,
to grant us this helper that we need
to exercise the priesthood that comes from the Apostles.

Grant, we pray, Almighty Father,
to this, your servant, the dignity of the priesthood;
renew deep within him
the Spirit of holiness;
may he henceforth possess this office
which comes from you, O God,
and is next in rank to the office of Bishop;
and by the example of his manner of life,
may he instill right conduct.

May he be a worthy co-worker with our Order,
so that **by his preaching**
and through the grace of the Holy Spirit
the words of the Gospel may bear fruit in human hearts
and reach even to the ends of the earth.

Together with us,
may he be a faithful steward of your mysteries,
so that your people may be renewed in the waters of rebirth
and nourished from your altar;
so that sinners may be reconciled
and the sick raised up.
May he be joined with us, Lord,

ORDINATION OF A PRIEST (ET 1975), *continued*

and the family of nations,
made one in Christ,
may become God's one, holy people.
We ask this through our Lord Jesus Christ, your Son,
who lives and reigns with you and the Holy Spirit,
one God, for ever and ever.
Amen.

ORDINATION OF PRIESTS (ET 2003), *continued*

in imploring your mercy
for the people entrusted to his care
and for all the world.

And so may the full number of the nations, gathered together in Christ,
be transformed into your one people
and made perfect in your Kingdom.
Through our Lord Jesus Christ, your Son,
who lives and reigns with you in the unity of the Holy Spirit,
God for ever and ever.
Amen.

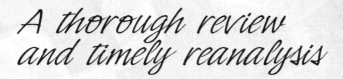